W9-CMM-132

Spices and New Worlds

Quests
for Spices
and New Worlds

Bertha S. Dodge

Archon Books 1988

Printed in the United States of America

The paper used in this publication meets the minimum
requirements of American National Standard for Information
Sciences-Permanence of Paper for Printed Library Materials,
ANSI 239.48-1984.

Library of Congress Cataloging-in-Publication Data

Dodge, Bertha Sanford, 1902–
    Quests for spices and new worlds / Bertha S. Dodge.
        p.   cm.
    Bibliography: p.
    Includes index.
    ISBN 0-208-02170-1
    1. Discoveries (in geography) 2. Spices. 3. Geography—
15th–16th
centuries. I. Title.
G95.D6   1988   910'.9'024—dc19   87-24192

Contents

Introduction

History is the story of people—their drives and their dreams. A central drive has been to dominate a never too friendly environment, accompanied by dreams of expanding such hard-won control. The difference between the drive and the dreams of our remotest ancestors—those for whom we have no records—and the less remote ones for whom we do have records is largely a matter of limits to risk taking imposed by ignorance and lack of skills. The only part of the environment those more distant ancestors could hope to exploit lay within the reach of their hands: the plants which might nourish them and the animals they might, if they were lucky, hunt successfully.

Men were, of course, taking risks when they tried unfamiliar plants but their needs outweighed the risks. Along the way, people were learning a great deal about plant uses beyond the possible food value. No one now knows when it was first perceived that some plant fibers could be twisted to form long threads and the threads further twisted into ropes or woven into textiles. We do not even know which dwellers in the high Andes first discovered that the bark of a tree growing there could assuage the fevers which attacked those rash enough to descend into adjacent tropical lowlands. Nor do we know when natives of the Brazilian jungles began to convert the sap of one kind of tree growing there into a product which a European chemist eventually baptized "rubber" and which would serve expanding civilizations in many ways. As awareness of such products grew, Europeans were moved to secure and transplant seeds and/or cuttings incidentally striving to control lands where such valued trees could be planted and mature.

The roles which quinine and rubber have played in human history can now hardly be questioned. The importance of some of the other plant products which men have sought to control is less compelling. In fact, it is hard to believe that today's world would be very different if the products of a large group of such plants never had been sought after and won. For though that heterogenous group called spices does add interesting flavors to foods and can further serve by concealing odors of decay, any reasons outside of material profit for their fatal lure to thousands upon thousands of Europeans of past centuries still remain far from convincing, at least as far as this writer is concerned.

What in no way remains obscure is the overpowering role such exotic plants have played in human affairs, and what a spur they provided to the discovery and exploration of new worlds.

1

Lure and Legend

It may well be that the value of spices to the Europeans of early centuries was enhanced by the mystery that long surrounded them. Whence did they originate? By whose agency and along what routes did they reach Alexandria, Egypt, where middlemen waited to secure them for markets farther to the west? Somewhere beyond in the Far East lay remote and fabled lands from which the spices came, journeying sometimes for years by caravans, being passed from one caravan to another with no caravan leader willing to disclose certain knowledge of the land of origin. Those orientals, however, were only too ready to enhance the market value of their products by accounting for them with fanciful tales whose inventiveness could do credit to the cherished stories of the *Thousand and One Nights*.

Whatever the motive, the quest for spices at their source dominated men's lives for centuries, even from biblical times when the Queen of Sheba brought appropriate bread-and-butter gifts to King Solomon on a camel caravan which "bare spices, and very much gold and precious stones."[1] Eleven hundred years after Sheba had torn herself from Solomon's embrace and during the first century of our era, when St. John was composing the Book of Revelation, spices remained an important item of exchange in the very commercial, very sinful city, Babylon the Great: "And the merchants of the earth shall weep and mourn over her, for no man bringeth their merchandise any more . . . the merchandise of gold and silver and precious stones . . . and cinnamon and colours and ointments."[2]

Romans had already encountered oriental commodities, notably silks, when, in 53 B.C., Roman legions came face-to-face with Parthians, ancestors of the Persians, present-day Iranians. Blinded by the brilliance of the silken banners the Parthians unfurled before them, Romans determined to have such silks for themselves. Roman officers guessed that somewhere beyond the land of these barbarians they were pursuing there must lie unknown lands sophisticated enough to fashion such amazing textiles and, just possibly, to produce other interesting commodities.

Once Romans had laid hands on some of those dazzling banners, they let it be known that they would be delighted to secure more of the same material. So, from their place practically astride the ancient silk road, the warlike Parthians perceived that, by becoming middlemen, they could win more than they had ever achieved by their notable feats of arms. Shrewdly guarding the secret as to exactly whence the coveted silks came, they would stimulate interest in other commodities to which the silk caravans gave them access. Roman trade in silks and spices so prospered that within seventy years silks were being purchased by Romans for their weight in gold. Spice values also soared and kept on soaring until by A.D. 410, the Visigoth king Alaric, who had just sacked Rome, was demanding that part of the ransom of that city be paid in pepper!

It was to be no flash in the pan—this valuing of a spice as ransom for an imperial city. Fourteen hundred years later, John Lothrop Motley, historian of seventeenth-century Holland, described the grim role another spice had played in the affairs of men: "It is wonderful to reflect upon the strange composition of man. The (European) world had lived in former ages very comfortably without cloves. But by the beginning of the seventeenth century that odoriferous pistil had been the cause of so many pitched battles and obstinate wars, of so much vituperating, negotiating, and intriguing, that the world's destiny seemed to have become almost dependent upon the growth of a particular gillyflower. Out of its sweetness had grown such bitterness among great nations as not torrents of blood could wash away. A commonplace enough condiment it seems to us now, easily to be dispensed with and not worth purchasing at a thousand lives a cargo, but it was once the great prize to be struggled for by civilized nations."[3] The same might have been written for other spices, notably cinnamon and pepper.

In search of lands where exotic plants grew native, men of centuries past were not only willing but eager to wager their lives first in seeking, then in seizing control, of those lands and in defending them against all comers. They even claimed sovereignty over the routes thither which their compatriots may have been the first to discover.

It is all but impossible to name any explorer of early centuries whose voyage was not financed either by an ambitious and greedy monarch or by a no less ambitious and greedy consortium of merchants, all financially interested in one or more products of the lands to be discovered. Neither sovereign nor merchants seemed to concern themselves with the lives sacrificed along the way. Each expedition being well supplied with men of God who were to offer unbaptized natives a new and sure way to salvation, the lives lost in the service of God, as well as of mammon, were assured immediate salvation. For the survivors there was more material profit. It was all a revised version of the twelfth-century Crusades, which sixteenth-century Europeans would have been well able to understand, and was linked to those earlier Crusades in more ways than one.

From the twelfth century onward, as crusading knights and their retinues trickled back into Europe after generally vain attempts to rescue the Holy Land from infidel hands, they brought in their baggage limited amounts of Eastern commodities and an unlimited taste for such commodities which, they had been told, came by long and devious routes from distant lands they had not seen. The hair-raising tales that were told of such routes suggest that the later estimate of a thousand lives per ship's cargo had been far outdistanced by the lives lost on long caravan crossings of the grimmest deserts and most forbidding mountain ranges of the whole world where, if the traveler managed to survive the pitilessness of nature, he might yet fall prey to scarcely less pitiless bandits.

At the western ends of these carvan routes were Mediterranean markets where merchants of many nationalities were waiting to purchase exotic articles at exotic prices. Ranking high among such markets were the ports of Antioch and Tyre in Asia Minor. Ranking higher still was Alexandria on the Nile Delta in Egypt. It mattered little to the multinational middlemen gathered in Alexandria whether their purchases had reached them wholly by a land route that angled down to cross the Isthmus of Suez or by a combination of sea and land routes. Arriving at some Red Sea port on a boat of undesignated land of origin, they were then transported on camels' backs on a short desert crossing to Cairo or Alexandria. It did, though, matter a great deal to the Persians who foresaw damage to their profitable roles as receivers and dispatchers of caravans. Soon they were spreading wild tales about the dangers of the sea route, thus temporarily deterring the fainthearted from attempting it, while suggesting nothing of the even grimmer dangers of alternate land routes.

These routes, baptized collectively the "ancient silk road," fanned out to encompass a number of Eastern lands. By these roads, oriental merchandise had reached imperial Rome from the far cities of imperial China. The total round trip, varying according to the particular branches of the road followed and the political and meteorological situation in lands being crossed, amounted to some 9,000 miles and could consume years of travel by caravan. A constant risk was the deserts to be passed over before reaching and crossing the "roof of the world"—those soaring mountain ranges that wall western China in.

The rewards seem to have outweighed the risks, for caravans did not desist from following the silk road. Edward Gibbon, historian of the late Roman Empire, described in some detail the various perils of that road and then described an alternate route from Samarcand (which is presently located in Soviet Asia just north of the Afghan border): "To escape the Tartar robbers and the tyrants of Persia, the silk caravans explored a more southern road; they traversed the mountains of Thibet, descended the streams of the Ganges and Indus and patiently expected, in the ports of Guzerat and Malabar, the annual fleets of the west."[4] Those "fleets of the west" were Arab dhows, taking on cargoes of spices as well as silks, which they would pay for with other spices destined to make the return journey to Samarcand, there to be transferred to yet other caravans, some headed for the western lands, some headed back into China, across the legendary deserts between.

As sinister as has been the reputation of the Gobi Desert, that of the more westerly Taklamakan is worse.

From marginal oasis to marginal oasis, slow-moving caravans advanced, hoping to complete the shortest crossing in a month. It is a region where time stands still and where the thirteenth-century comments of the Venetian Marco Polo could equally well be applied to any century since (until, in recent decades, a hard-surfaced road has been laid out). Then, as now, searingly hot by day, bitterly cold by night, without landmarks other than shifting sand dunes, the desert won for itself a reputation as the abode of evil spirits who "amuse travellers" to their destruction with most extraordinary illusions.[5] Such spirits were said to summon the unwary to step aside from the moving caravan and be lost, or to trap entire caravans into moving in circles.

With or without such evil spirits, the deserts of western China had not noticeably changed by the 1920s when a British consul residing at a large oasis city near the Taklamakan described the view from Goma at the desert's margin. "To the north in the clear dawn the view is inexpressively awe-inspiring and sinister. The yellow dunes of the Taklamakan, like the great waves of a petrified ocean, extend in countless myriads to the far horizon, with here and there an extra large sand-hill, a king dune as it were, towering above its fellows. They seem to clamor silently, those dunes, for travellers to engulf, for whole caravans to swallow up as they have swallowed so many in the past."[6]

So much for the clear view! But suddenly the sky might grow dark and in a moment a storm could burst upon the traveller—a black hurricane "like Hell let loose," as another traveller expressed it. He added that any traveller overwhelmed by such a storm must, in spite of the heat, entirely envelop himself in felts to escape injury from stones dashing around with a mad force that required that both men and horses lie down and endure the rage of the sometimes hours-long hurricane. The noise from the storm-driven stones could be deafening.

Ever unhappily aware of threatening hurricanes and evil spirits, haunted by thirst, and frequently reminded by human and animal skeletons of how their own journey might end, caravans laden with highly saleable nonessentials continued to pass that way, the merchants deterred only as death might intervene or bandits rush down upon them. Small wonder that surviving caravan merchants demanded high prices for the merchandise they finally succeeded in offering for sale in western markets!

Though not listed on any bills of lading, not the least interesting of the commodities that journeyed along the ancient silk road were the insubstantial ones—the bits and pieces of information that helped build up in European minds pictures of a romantic East, giving birth to numberless and often fantastic legends about the lands whence came those silks and spices. Such legends, recorded in part and further circulated by word of mouth, may seem completely unbelievable to us, yet perhaps no more so than today's tales of little green men from Mars may seem to people of ages to come. Documents embodying such legends seem to have formed the escape literature of those uncertain times. Life, ever threatened by famine, pestilence and war, was precarious and men longed to believe that somewhere beyond their own confining horizons lay bright and wondrous lands.

One such fabulous land was the kingdom of an immensely rich, wise, and apparently immortal monarch who, being a humble Christian in faith, was said to disavow all royal titles to call himself simply "Prester John"—Priest John. For a long time it was supposed that Prester John reigned in India, but when Europeans finally reached India and found no such monarch there, they blithely transferred his realm to Africa, specifically to Abyssinia (Ethiopia) where the famous Queen of Sheba had once reigned. The only unchallengeable truth of the Prester John legend was that the Abysinians were Christians, belonging to the Coptic Church.

There is in the possession of the Vatican a letter supposedly sent by Prester John, in the year 1122, to the Pope and curia, who had requested information concerning his kingdom. Long recognized as a forgery, the letter is an amazing document, though no less so than the fact that it ever was taken seriously. It runs, in part: "If, indeed, you wish to know the greatness and excellence of our majesty and what countries are subject to our lordship, understand and believe without doubt that, as Prester John, I am lord of lords. I surpass under heaven in riches and virtue and power all other kings who are upon the whole earth. Seventy-two kings are our tributaries. . . . Our magnificence surpasses all the wealth that is in the world."[7] The reputedly humble priest-king continues presenting wonders like gold-digging ants the size of young dogs and two-headed serpents and forests of pepper trees—the latter, at least, being a real possibility. Because of such tales, the very occasional European traveller who took the overland route to the East would not only seek Prester John's kingdom but also Prester John in person.

For an imaginative man like the almost-as-legendary travel writer, Sir John Mandeville (1300?–1372?), Prester John's letter was to form the basis for all sorts of tall tales and fabulous creatures—one-eyed monsters (possibly cribbed from the ancient cyclops legend) and sciapods, amazing humanoid creatures with only a single, very large foot each, upon which they hopped about in lively fashion and which, when they wished to relax in the sun, they could raise over their heads like a parasol.

When, in 1295, after an absence of twenty-five years, the Polos—Nicolo, Maffeo, and Marco—finally returned to Venice, shabbily clad and speaking their native tongue haltingly, such old associates as were still alive viewed them as impostors. Only after they had ripped up the linings of their shabby clothes to reveal fortunes in jewels were Venetians persuaded to accept them as long-lost fellow citizens. When the Polos told questioning friends of the further rich commodities of the far lands they had traversed, they were hardly believed. They would have been more enthusiastically received had they told of sciapods.

In addition to the jewels, whose reality could not be questioned, the Polos told of pepper, nutmegs, spikenard, cubebs, cloves and all other valuable spices which occasion it (Java) to be visited by many ships."[8] Ships! Maritime-minded Venetians were bound to wonder to what nation those ships belonged. Why should there not be among them ships from Europe, specifically from Venice? So far, no European ships were believed to have made the voyage but men were unwilling to accept the idea that none ever could. Europe was not to resign itself meekly and indefinitely to receiving coveted Eastern commodities by land routes which terminated at the eastern end of the Mediterranean where Moslem traders must be dealt with.

The radical idea of ships sent from Europe must have begun to dawn well before the Polos had set forth on their journey into China and it surely would have gathered momentum had not all books then been even rarer and costlier than oriental merchandise. Rabbi Benjamin of Tudela's book about his thirteen-year (1160–1173) tour of the less remote East would then have been widely read, had it been available. Of the flourishing international markets on an island called Kish in the Persian Gulf, he wrote that there "the traders of Mesopotamia, Yemen, and Persia import all silk and purple cloths, flax, cotton, hemp, mash, wheat . . . those from India import great quantities of spices. . . . Seven days distant is Chulam. . . . Pepper grows in this country; the trees which bear the fruit are planted in the fields, which surround the town. . . . Cinnamon and many other spices grow in this country.[9] Another traveller, a Friar Odoric, reported that on an island called Java grew spices like cloves and nutmegs (the Spice Islands themselves being as yet unknown). Had Friar Odoric actually visited Java or was he just passing on gossip?

For people who had read or been told of such travelogues, the evidence seemed to point to rich pickings in the East if only they could find their way there in ships which could load return cargoes of spices. The friendliness of Far Eastern peoples being uncertain, a Christian monarch like Prester John could prove to be an important ally—if only they could find him and arrange an appropriate treaty!

2

Priest Potentate John

Even before the year 1498, when the Portuguese Vasco da Gama managed to locate a sea route east, King John of Portugal (Dom João) had arranged for scouts to find Prester John's kingdom and report on it and its ruler. One such scout, Pero de Covilham, after a roundabout journey that took several years, finally reached Ethiopia, and there so ingratiated himself with the reigning "Prester John," whose actual name was Lebna Dengel, that he was denied permission to leave again for home.

From Father Francisco Alvares, who kept a journal of a slightly later official Portuguese mission to this Prester John—a mission that was finally allowed to return home—we get a fascinating picture both of the fabled kingdom and of the kind of life being lived there by the mission and by that fifteenth-century displaced person, Pero de Covilham. The mission of which Father Alvares was a member left Portugal in 1515, reaching Portuguese India in 1517 and, after a considerable delay in Goa, sailed west again for nearly 2,000 miles across the Indian

Ocean to reach the Ethiopian port of Massawa in 1520.
For the next six years, the mission followed Prester John
as his court kept continually on the move. In spite of
physical hardships and the numberless frustrations involved, Father Alvares faithfully recorded all he saw and
heard. His account is refreshingly free from one-eyed
monsters, two-headed serpents, and sciapods.

In the land of Prester John, pepper seems to have
wielded hardly less power than the king himself. Nothing could be done there without pepper, either as bribes
or for the outright purchase of commodities. At a town
named Barua, for instance, when they went to visit an
important official on his invitation, "we found there men
like porters, each with his whip in his hand, saying we
should give them some pepper, and they kept us for a
good while at the gate." At Ingabelu, "we found in this
town an infinite quantity of fowls, of which 100 could be
bought at leisure, if one wanted so many, in exchange
for a little pepper, so little do they value the hens and so
highly do they value pepper."[1]

When Lebna Dengel's courtiers demanded more
generous gifts of pepper for their sovereign, the ambassador tried to explain that "because money was not
current in this kingdom, on that account the Captain
Major [in India] of the King of Portugal had given him,
besides much gold and silver, much pepper and cloth for
their expenses, and of this pepper which he had brought
for his expenditures, he had already given four bales to
the Prester." A strange court for a king of "surpassing
magnificence"!

Finally, after long, drawn-out dickerings to little
purpose, Prester John gave his royal consent for the
Portuguese mission to depart. They had to wait until
some Portuguese vessel should stop by the Abyssinian
port of Massawa on the voyage home from India. The
vessel arrived there in 1526 and in 1527, after an absence
of over ten years, the surviving mission members

reached Portugal, though bringing none of the splendid achievements that had been anticipated.

Pero de Covilham did not even try to leave with his fellow Portuguese. A man of extraordinary facility with languages and, further, a talent for conversing entertainingly in several of them, he was not a man from whom Prester John would willingly part. Showered by Lebna Dengel with honors and riches, and knowing that the successor to the Portuguese king who had sent him forty years before as a secret agent might not feel inclined to reward him, Pero de Covilham made no effort to leave with his compatriots. Father Alvares parted from him reluctantly.

Had any of the information secret agent Pero de Covilham tried to send out to his king ever reached Portugal? According to what Pero told Father Alvares, he had tried to smuggle out information in a letter entrusted to a merchant headed north. No copy of such a letter now survives in the Portuguese archives, but if it had reached the king, it could have stimulated interest in locating a sea route to India. In any case, the time was soon to come when the Moorish middlemen who had dominated the markets of the eastern Mediterranean for so long would have to adjust to a new set of realities.

Whatever they may have looked like, world maps, such as the one given by the Portuguese king to Pero de Covilham to help guide him to his destination, and the somewhat later one sent as a gift to Prester John with the second Portuguese mission, would bear scant resemblance to any map of our own century. Concepts of geography were then only slightly advanced over the sixth-century ones described by Edward Gibbon: "The Christian geography was forcibly extracted from the texts of scripture, and the study of nature was the surest symptom of an unbelieving mind. The orthodox faith confined the habitable world to one temperate zone and represented the earth as an oblong surface, four hundred days journey in length and two hundred in breadth, encompassed with ocean, and covered by the solid crystal of the firmament."[2] Under the circumstances, to as much as hint that the earth might actually be a globe— as, since antiquity, a few impious heathen had dared suggest—was nothing short of blasphemy.

During the following nine centuries, man's conception of the world slowly expanded and became accepted. Yet in the late fifteenth century, a great many empty spaces remained on the map. Africa, south of the Sahara, was then a blank so total that one of Pero de Covilham's charges had been to locate an all-water route connecting the all-but-unknown west coast of Africa with the then completely unknown kingdom of Prester John.

Beyond Asia Minor and the coastal fringes of Arabia, Persia, and India, Asia remained generally unknown despite Marco Polo's revelations. Australia had never even been dreamed of and the polar regions were so little understood that in the eighteenth century navigators were still expecting to find a balmy continent in the far, far south. America was yet to be discovered when Pero de Covilham set forth and even by the time of the later mission to Prester John, all that was yet known of America (not so named until later) was a handful of off-shore islands and a thin shell of coastline. Any fifteenth-century map had to be a crude affair despite the beautifully and elaborately drawn embellishments around the edge, none so much as hinting at a navigable route to the lands of silks and spices.

Any knowledge as to where those exotic lands lay was a secret closely guarded by people in the know. This was achieved not by outright refusal to discuss such matters but by deliberately fabricated fantastic tales that, through the centuries, had added interest and value to the subject. This ruse was perceived by Pliny the Elder as early as the first century A.D. He wrote: "In regard to cinnamon and casia, a fabulous story has been related by antiquity, and first of all by Herodotus [about 484–420 B.C.] that they are obtained from birds' nests, and particularly that of the phoenix and that they are knocked down from inaccessible rocks and trees by the weight of the flesh brought there by the birds themselves, or by means of arrows loaded with lead; and similarly there is a tale of casia growing round marshes under the protection of a terrible kind of bats which guard it with their claws, and of winged serpents—those tales being invented by the natives to raise the price of their commodities."[3]

However raised, gathered, and transported, such commodities were destined for those Mediterranean ports where East met and bargained with West. However much greedy and adventurous merchants may have stretched out to the fringes of the known world, the center as far as navigators and trade were concerned— for European merchants, at least—long remained that *mare nostrum* or "our sea" of classical times, the Mediterranean. This sea was generally navigated by shore-hugging vessels, rarely crossed by routes that took ships out of sight of land for long, in voyages sponsored by merchant-seafarers of ports like Venice or Genoa or Marseilles. During the 1160s, Rabbi Benjamin of Tudela noted that Alexandria afforded an excellent market to men of all nations, of which he enumerated about thirty as being present there. Few on his list were larger than the city-states of Italy. Portugal, presently to become a mercantile power to be reckoned with, was not even mentioned.

An unidentified ship's captain of the late 1500s reported to Richard Hakluyt: "Alexandria in Egypt is a free port, and when a man commeth within the castels, presently the Ermyn sends abord to have one come and speake with him, to know what goods are abord the shippe, to see all the goods discharged. And then from the Ermine you goe to the Bye, onely that he will inquire news of you, and so from thence to the Consuls house where you lye. The Venetians have a Consul themselves. But all other nations goe to the French nations Consul, who will give you a chamber for your selves, if you will so have it." For "his aide, and meate and drinke and all,"⁴ that consul was to be paid two percent, presumably computed on the business his guest had transacted there.

After discussing saleable commodities, prices, and exchange rates, the captain explains: "Commonly the Caravans come thither in October from Mecca to Cairo, and from thence to Alexandria, where the merchants be that buy the spices."⁵ Prices per quintal [approximately a hundredweight] were quoted for pepper and ginger, though how to equate them to today's weights and currencies remains a mystery.

During those centuries when Alexandria dominated the Mediterranean spice trade, European Christians could not have found Moslem Egypt altogether congenial, isolated as they were in their national enclaves. This they endured, seeing their rewards in the prices their wares might bring in home markets. A further handicap for them was that they had to buy spices unsorted as they were shipped from the spice lands, whereas European mercantile houses demanded spices already sorted by size and quality. Thus the European trader in Alexandria had to have a sound instinct as to when and to what extent he was being cheated and to balance that against the probable more-than-hundred percent profit to be made in Europe. Finally, he must decide whether it could all be worth the personal insults and humiliations he had been made to endure. If such traders dreamed of one day bypassing Alexandrian markets in favor of dealing directly with the Far East, it is hardly to be wondered at. Knowing that land routes to the East were dangerous, Moslem-dominated, and frequently brigand-infested, they had to be thinking in terms of someone, somehow finding a sea route there. But where exactly were the lands, and how to find them?

Human nature being what it is and human beings being by nature restless and inquisitive, it is now a bit hard to understand why so many centuries passed before men began to try filling in those great blank spaces on the maps of the world. To be just, there were valid excuses. Navigation long remained a crude art though generally adequate for Mediterranean voyages. Sailing the great ocean, however, was a totally different matter. Days and weeks could pass without sighting a landmark to steer by. Steering by the stars demanded that the stars be visible—something that could not be counted on in wide and stormy seas. Longitude was then a matter of dead reckoning and guess. A familiarity with currents and the habits of birds, as well as of the seaweed that might float by, could give a pilot some idea of where his ship might be, but he could equally well have no idea of where he was and in what direction he should be sailing.

The difficulties were compounded by lingering strange beliefs about the unknown parts of the world. An Arabian contemporary of Marco Polo wrote of that world: "No one knows what lies beyond in the Atlantic; no one has been able to discover anything for certain, on account of the difficulties of navigation, due to the darkness, the height of the waves, the frequency of the tempests, and the violence of the winds."[6] Others had written: "In that sea are places where flames of fire, a hundred cubits high, perpetually rise into the air. Here, too, are enormous fishes of great length."[7] Great whales and volcanoes spouting fire, as on the Cape Verde Islands and the Azores, could be terrifying to superstitious men who witnessed such things for the first time.

Of course, fable and fact were strangely mixed. "In this sea is an island where, in a castle of surpassing beauty, the body of King Solomon is to be found."[8] For mariners who couldn't care less about where King Solomon's body might lie and whose only active interest in that monarch would have been to locate his mines, the Atlantic must long remain a sea to be avoided. There had to be some special persuasion for any mariner to take the risk.

But for lands like England, Spain, and Portugal which faced this wider sea, wilder than the Mediterranean, whose confines were yet to be determined, various possibilities must have come to mind. Some land might lie beyond that sea in the far, unseen, unexplored distance. Might it not be that the same ocean of darkness whose waves beat so violently on Cape St. Vincent jutting out from the southwest corner of Portugal, also beat on some far shore that might or might not be as formidable as claimed by the ancients?

Unless someone found a way to overcome doubts and fears, as well as the formidable difficulties of navigation, lands like England and Spain and Portugal must resign themselves to very circumscribed roles on the stage of history and thus remain poor dependents on the bounty of other nations with which they could not always hope to remain at peace. The sea had to be their destiny.

This maritime destiny was particularly urgent in Portugal, frequently cut off from land communication with the remainder of Europe for, in spite of a shared Latin heritage, Portugal and the land along its northeast border—Spain—were often in direct conflict and rarely completely at peace. So Portugal was forced to keep open sea routes with other European lands where her trade was to be carried on. And keeping sea routes open meant developing seafaring skills like shipbuilding and navigation and mapmaking. The development of such skills and of the men who could practice them meant, in turn, providing some means for those men to exercise those skills as well as the motivation to keep them honed.

3

Prince-Navigator and Neophytes

For the lands of the Iberian Peninsula which had lain for hundreds of years under Moorish dominion, there was even more explicit motivation for outflanking Moorish merchants than for other European lands. During the twelfth and thirteenth centuries the Crusades offered any Christian who helped to wrest heathen lands from the control of Moors the certainty of winning credit in heaven and on earth, particularly if he added to his feats of arms the conversion of heathen to Christianity. Even though the Moors themselves were not likely to be converted, the Crusaders could still possibly find credit in humbling those proud people in any way possible.

Much had been learned about the Near East during the centuries when the knights of Europe set forth with their retinues of retainers to redeem the Holy Land from infidel hands. There, whatever the ultimate success of their avowed purpose, they were to be "conquered" by Far Eastern commodities, notably the finer textiles of cotton and silk. They discovered paper manufactured from cotton, thus paving the way for books other than the few laboriously written on parchment. Rice, sugar, lemons, and, not least, spices were increasingly known to them and desired. The demand for such exotic products returned with them to Europe. Inevitably, there grew proportionate dreams and schemes of making direct contact with the lands whence came the coveted commodities.

Still more significant was their exposure to the Arabian devices which the Crusaders presently appropriated despite a Church interdiction of them as inventions of the Evil One. There was, for instance, the earliest form of the compass, a magnetized needle bound to a splinter of wood which could be floated on water and turn to point towards the magnetic north. There was the astrolabe, a Moorish invention, which gave a mariner who had lost sight of land a means to determine his latitude. There were also Arabian geographies and maps which not even the devoutest of mariners totally rejected. It was such devices that would help make it possible, after the last Crusader had given up and returned home, for his descendants to become conquerors of the open seas and find their way to the Far East—and back.

Portuguese navigators, seeking that way east, could not ignore an apparently insurmountable barrier to the south—the African continent whose southern limits they did not know. Yet for men who had access to ancient tales, there seemed a hint that Africa had in fact been circumnavigated. Writing of "Libya," by which he meant the whole of Africa, and of the "Phoenicians," by which he probably meant those Phoenician colonists, the Carthaginians, Herodotus described a voyage that took place a century prior to his writing. "It is certain that Libya is surrounded by sea, except where it is joined to Asia, and the first to demonstrate this, as far as we know, was the Egyptian king Necos. . . . He dis-

patched certain Phoenicians on a voyage, and bade them
to sail so as to come home between the Pillars of Heracles
[Straits of Gibraltar]. . . . The Phoenicians set out from
the Red Sea and sailed the southern sea; as often as
autumn came, they went ashore and sowed the land in
whatever part of Libya they had reached in their voyage
and waited for the harvest; when they gathered the crop
and sailed on. Thus two years passed, and in the third
year they turned through the Pillars of Heracles and
reached Egypt. They said what to me is unbelievable,
though some may believe it: that as they sailed round
Libya they had the sun on their right hand."[1] That is,
they sailed to the north, which was something not even
the credulous Herodotus could swallow.

This was a feat not surpassed, probably not even
equalled, for nearly 2,000 years, possibly because men
were attempting to round Africa in the opposite direction, a far more difficult voyage. The Portuguese king,
however, may have had Herodotus's account in mind
when he so hopefully sent out Pero de Covilham,
charged not only with finding the land of Prester John
but also with locating an all-water passage across Africa.
He may have suspected that the wily Phoenicians had
found and used such a passage.

Already a century before Pero set forth, another
Portuguese king had become sufficiently aware of the
value of a navy to encourage shipbuilding by supplying
timber from royal forests and by forgoing customs duties
on shipbuilding supplies like iron and tar. A maritime
insurance company was started and no export duty was
to be levied on the first voyage of any Portuguese-built
ship. In order to expand Lisbon into a world mart, King
Ferdinand I offered special privileges to foreign merchants, thus luring them, as well as skilled foreign
navigators, to his capital. It was an atmosphere meant to
encourage navigators of the kind that eventually dared
face the dangers of the dreaded "Sea of Darkness."

The moving spirit behind continuation of this development was a non-navigating navigator, a young prince whom his father (King John, successor to Ferdinand) put in charge of the nation's African affairs. Later to be known as "Prince Henry the Navigator," he would earn his reputation not by going to sea himself but by inspiring and supporting a generation of navigators. Yet even had there been no Prince Henry, there might have been some other men to push Portugal into the new age of exploration or, more precisely, of commercial expansion. The time was ripe and Portugal was fortunate in having the right attributes assembled in a man who possessed the power and authority to follow dreams so advanced for the times.

It was his royal heritage that gave Prince Henry not only the status to lead but power to achieve. He began by distinguishing himself as a soldier—a matter of great importance in an age of chivalry—in planning the capture, in 1415, of Ceuta, a Moorish stronghold and trading center on the African coast opposite Gibraltar. Having earned thereby the respect of the nobles, he would thenceforth have their cooperation as well as that of humbler seamen. For his doughty deeds, his father, King John, made him Duke of Viseu and Lord of Covilham, adding presently an appointment as grand master of the Order of Christ. This would give him access to the order's funds which he could then tap in pursuit of his dream.

That dream, so appropriate for a grand master of the Order of Christ, was to include finding, then trading with remote heathen lands, hopefully converting the inhabitants to Christianity and, incidentally, humiliating the unconvertable Mohammedans wherever and however that might be achieved. It was further expected that in exotic lands such as were proposed for investigation, the navigators would be able to reimburse themselves the cost of the voyages with the proceeds realized from gold, silver, jewels, and spices those lands would yield.

In Prince Henry there were combined personal qualities required for the realization of his dream. A medieval knight hovering on the brink of the Renaissance, he lived a life totally exemplary by the standards of his times and died at the age of sixty-six, in 1460, much admired both for this leadership of a coterie of navigators and for the hair shirt found next his skin at the time of his death.

The war against the infidel was a sort of tit-for-tat long carried out between Arabs and the Portuguese, whose ships, flaunting a large red cross on each white sail, were not always easily distinguished from pirate ships. "After the taking of Ceuta," a contemporary chronicler records of his deeply admired prince, "he always kept ships well armed against the Infidel, both for war and because he had also a wish to know the land that lay beyond the isles of Canary and that Cape called Bojador, for that up to his time, neither by writings, nor by the memory of man, was known with any certainty what lay beyond that Cape. . . . And because the said Lord Prince wished to know the truth of this,—since it seemed to him that if he or some other lord did not endeavour to gain that knowledge, no mariners or merchants would ever dare to attempt it—(for it is clear that none of them ever trouble themselves to sail to a place where there is not a sure and certain hope of profit)."[2]

The mercantile impulse (a compelling addition to the "wish to know"), is enlarged in the following paragraph: "The second reason was that if there chanced to be in those lands some population of Christians, or some havens, into which it would be possible to sail without peril, many kinds of merchandise might be brought to this realm, which would find a ready market, and reasonably so, because no other people of these parts traded with them . . . and also the products of this realm might be taken there, which traffic would bring great profit to our countrymen."[3]

The third reason was to find out how far into Africa the power of the Moors extended. The fourth reason followed from the third "because during the one and thirty years that he had warred against the Moors, he had never found a Christian king, nor a lord outside this land, who for the love of our Lord Jesus Christ would aid him in the said war . . . against those enemies of the faith."[4] The fifth reason given was, of course, the evangelization of the heathen. The sixth and final reason seems to have been a purely astrological one which suggested that the prince was predestined to success.

A contemporary portrait of that prince shows a man with a dour expression on his long face and eyes that reveal none of the fire that must have accompanied the driving force behind his passion for searching out new lands. The admiring chronicler tells of the rising sun finding him seated where it had left him the day before, his taking little rest, and spending much of his time with people of "many nationalities." Prince Henry's greatest strength—unappreciated, of course, by the contemporary biographer—lay just in the fact that in a highly bigoted and close-minded age he managed to maintain a sufficiently broad-minded outlook to welcome to his modest court at Sagres any and all men who might help in the realization of his goal. There were mariners of all nations, Jewish mapmakers, Moors with their advanced knowledge of mathematics and of medicine as well as those of remoter lands upon which the prince was focusing. Of the Portuguese at his court, there were a large sprinkling of men at arms and outright adventurers, sons of poor nobility who could not hope to advance in the contemporary world without performing notable feats of arms. In a world that was briefly at peace, they sought other means to win renown and fortune.

Although Prince Henry "sent out many times, not

only ordinary men, but such as by their experience in great deeds of war were of the foremost name in the profession of arms, yet there was not one who dared to pass that Cape of Bojador and learn about the land beyond it . . . this was not from cowardice or want of good will, but . . . from the wide-spread and ancient rumour about this Cape, that had been cherished by the mariners from Spain from generation to generation. . . . How are we, men said, to pass the bounds that our fathers set up."[5] They would certainly be risking soul as well as body by becoming "wilful murderers of themselves."

"For, said the mariners, this much is clear, that beyond this Cape there is no race of men nor place of inhabitants . . . while the currents are so terrible that no ship having once passed the Cape will ever be able to return."[6] Men of their times—devout, superstitious, deeply imbued with those ancient legends about the "Sea of Darkness"—there were yet some intelligent and skilled enough to master the developing art and science of navigation, to learn to use the crude contemporary compass and astrolabe and to interpret such charts as were available. Eventually some proved to be brave enough and loyal enough to their prince to follow his commands to keep on sailing south until they had passed all previously known capes, even the menacing one called Bojador. But it would take time for this to come about.

The Portuguese chronicler Gomes Eannes de Azurara saw Spain as the villain behind the grim legends which he believed were being spread in order to discourage Portuguese mariners from undertaking profitable explorations. The seeds of international rivalry in exploration were already beginning to sprout.

Constantly reminded of those dangers, Prince Henry rejected them. Buoyed by an inner certainty, he continued to insist that no cape could be so fearsome that brave men could not pass beyond it. Perhaps only a man of his conspicuous abilities—extraordinarily disciplined, self-denying, whole-heartedly dedicated to enhancing his country's prestige and mercantile power, as well as to spreading the Christian faith among heathen—could have succeeded in persuading anyone to undertake a voyage aimed at passing an unpassable cape.

It was not until 1443, five years after Prince Henry had set up his court at Sagres, that his first objective was achieved through the agency of his young equerry, Gil Eannes. But it took two voyages. On the first, Eannes and his men became "touched by the self-same terror" and returned without success. The next year, "despising all danger," he tried again and succeeded in passing beyond Cape Bojador to find there a land no more forbidding than that to the north of the cape. Seeing rosemary growing there in the sands, he plucked a spray to take back to his royal sponsor.

One of the prince's later biographers summed it up tellingly, saying that with that rosemary a whole era of superstition fell away—much as the sand cliffs along that coast may collapse and disappear without a trace into the ocean. For more than just a forbidding cape had been passed. Also passed was a milestone in human thought and vision. Cape after African cape were soon passed, with ships of newly courageous courtiers meeting and bartering with the natives, bringing back to Portugal cargoes of ever-increasing value—gold dust, ivory, wax, skins, sugar, and that Malaguetta "pepper" whose spicy seeds, many insisted, were no less desirable than the more familiar pepper of the Spice Islands (though botanically more closely related to cardamon). Unfortunately, those trading ships also brought back blacks purchased from Arab slave traders or from native tribes with whom the slaves' tribes happened to be at war and whom devout sons of the Church looked upon ambiguously as pagan souls to be saved and strong bodies to be exploited.

As he glanced over his shoulder toward Spain, the prince realized that rival European nations must soon learn of the profits being made and would try to get possession of lands from which such profits came. Lest his country be excluded from the trade her navigators had established at so great a cost in money and lives, Prince Henry sent an embassy to the pope, begging the pontiff, in whose person seemed to be embodied a sort of league of nations, to issue a decree stating that lands discovered by Portuguese navigators should belong to Portugal or at least be considered under Portuguese rule. The natives were not consulted either by prince or pope.

The pope, Eugenius IV (1380–1447), a Venetian who had reached his papal eminence in 1431, granted Prince Henry's request, adding "a plenary indulgence for the souls of such as should perish in the undertaking." Thus the seizure of newly discovered lands was officially raised to the level of a Crusade. Realization would be long in coming that the profit motive thus stimulated threatened more lives more grimly than ever had the bloody hand-to-hand battles between the earlier Crusaders and the Saracens.

Under Prince Henry's urging, cape after African cape was passed until by the time he died in 1460, his mariners were starting on a southeasterly direction towards the Bight of Benin. Though not yet quite half the way towards the southernmost cape of all, the sailors were happily congratulating themselves that this eastern trend was soon to take them round the end of the continent and into the seas men had so long been reaching for. It would, however, be another quarter-century after the prince-navigator had passed away before the Cape of Good Hope would be reached, named, and passed. During this quarter-century, Portuguese mariners were becoming increasingly knowledgeable about the west coast of Africa—the Guinea coast, as it was called. But exactly where those heirs of Henry's dream dropped anchor and what kind of trade they carried on there was, insofar as possible, kept a national secret.

4

The World Divided

It was in the summer of 1487 that King John of Portugal, finally purged of his reluctance to encourage what he had viewed as Prince Henry's mad and costly schemes, sent forth the caravel *São Cristovão*, with two accompanying caravels, under the command of Bartolomeu Dias. Dias was directed to seek out the kingdom of Prester John from the sea as Pero de Covilham had been instructed to do by a land route. The vessels kept sailing south and in January 1488, pushed from behind by a heavy northwest gale, lost sight of land. When they regained it, they found that as they sailed north the land was on the *left* hand. Without having been aware of it, they had sailed round the southernmost tip of Africa!

About 200 miles beyond, the seamen, sick with scurvy and exhausted by the unremitting labors of trying to keep the vessel afloat and on course in storm-lashed seas, refused to continue their struggle. To cover his failure to pursue further discoveries, Dias took a vote of all on board and, with this unanimously in favor of abandoning the voyage, turned back for home. On the return voyage he called at the cape which the storm had prevented him from visiting on the outward voyage, naming it *Cabo da Boa Esperança*—Cape of Good Hope.

By late December, Dias's caravels came proudly sailing up the Tagus River to drop anchor off Lisbon. Dias went immediately to pay his respects to the king— an audience reported by a Genoese mariner who happened to be present at the interview and who jotted down a description of it in a marginal note he inscribed in his personal copy of a world geography: "Note that in this year '88 in the month of December arrived in Lisbon *Bartolomeus Didacus* captain of three caravels which the most serene king of Portugal had sent out to try the land of Guinea. He reported . . . that he had reached a promontory which he called *Cabo de Boa Esperança*, which we believe to be Agesinha [Abyssinia]. He says that in this place he discovered by the astrolabe that he was 45° below the equator. He has described his voyage and plotted it league by league on a marine chart in order to place it under the eyes of the said king. I was present in all of this."[1] Today we know that that Cape lies at 34°21' south—which goes to underline the kind of observations a fifteenth-century navigator had to rely upon.

The writer of the above marginal note was one Christopher Columbus, in Lisbon trying to persuade the Portuguese monarch, as he was presently to try with the English and eventually the Spanish, to underwrite his proposed voyage to the Far East. He based his far-too-optimistic computations of the distance there on a contemporary miscalculation of the actual length of a degree on the earth's surface at the latitude he planned to follow. Dias's return to Lisbon after rounding Africa put an end to the king's interest in Columbus, for whose services he believed he could have no further use.

Columbus already had other strings to his bow,

other directions in which to look for support. There was a strong stimulus coming from the growing international rivalries for trade with the East. Bartholomew Columbus had already been spending considerable time at the court of Henry VII of England, trying to solicit support there for his brother's proposed voyage. Christopher's son Fernando, in his biography of his father, was to describe his uncle's efforts, later lifted and published in translation in Hakluyt's *Principal Navigations:*

> Christopher Columbus fearing lest the king of Castile in like maner (as the king of Portingall had done) should not condescend unto his enterprise, he should be inforced to offer the same againe to some other prince, and so much time should be spent therein, sent into England a certaine brother of his which he had with him, whose name was Bartholomew Columbus, who, albeit he had not the Latine tongue, yet nevertheless was a man of experience and skilfull in sea causes, and could very well make sea cards and globes, and other instruments belonging to that profession, as he was instructed by his brother. Wherfore after that Bartholomew was departed for England, his lucke was to fall into the hands of pirats, which despoiled him with the rest of them that were in the ship which he went in. Upon which occasion, and by reason of his poverty and sicknesse which cruelly assaulted him in a country so far distant from his friends, he deferred his ambassage for a long while, until such time as he had gotten somewhat handsome about him with the making of sea cards. At length he began to deale with king Henry the seventh the father of Henry the eight, which reigneth at this present: unto whom he

presented a mappe of the world. . . . But to
return to the king of England, I say that after
he had seene the map, & that which my father,
Christopher Columbus offered unto him, he
accepted the offer with joyfull countenance,
and sent to call him into England. But because
God had reserved the said offer for Castile,
Columbus was gone in the meane space, and
also returned with the performance of his enterprise.[2]

The race to the Spice Islands was gathering momentum and King Henry VII, deprived of Columbus's "enterprise," turned to another Genoese, whom he mistak-
enly called Venetian, of the family name Caboto. In
1495, King Henry issued to "John Cabot" letters patent
"for the discoverie of new and unknowne lands." The
letter ran, in part:

Be it known that we have given and granted
. . . to our welbeloved John Cabot citizen of
Venice, to Lewis, Sebastian & Santius sonnes
of said John, and to the heyres of them and
theyr deputies, full and free authority, leave,
and power to saile to all parts, countries and
seas of the East, of the West, and of the North,
under our banners and ensignes, with five ships
of what burthen or quantity soever they be,
and as many mariners or men as they will have
with them in sayd ships, upon their owne
proper costs and charges, to seeke out, discover, and finde whatsoever isles, countries,
regions or provinces of the heathen which before this time have been unknowen to all Christians: we have given them licence to set up our
banners and ensignes in every village, towne,
castle, isle or maine land of them newly found
. . .[3]

Clearly, it was intended that John Cabot and his sons were, at their own expense, to subdue, occupy, and possess in the name of this typically stingy sovereign, lands from which they might possibly reimburse themselves but only after they had returned bringing valuable cargoes on which King Henry VII would graciously remit customs duties. The king, risking no more than paper and ink, was to receive, after the Cabots had deducted the costs of the voyage, "one fifth part of the capitall gaine so gotten."

John Cabot's voyages achieved no more than the possible sighting of a northern coast of what might be a new continent. The Portuguese king was duly alarmed, realizing that he had missed out on the sponsorship of that continent by terminating his dealings with Columbus once Dias had returned with his own great news. Columbus's "performance of his enterprise" under the sponsorship of the sovereigns of Castile and León would have been a bitter pill for the Portuguese king, who did not know whether the new continent might yield his rival monarchs spices, or at least easy access to spice lands. Were the lands his navigators had won at such great cost, to the profit of king and country, to be preempted by those greedy neighbors, the Spanish?

The Spanish monarchs were equally determined not only to hold what had been discovered in voyages they had sponsored, but to continue pursuing the same course until their mariners should have arrived at the fabled Spice Islands, making them the property of the discoverer's sponsoring land. Distressed by the realization of what he had rejected and allowed to go by default to his rival, Spain, King John determined to make as certain as possible that what his own navigators had won and might further win should not get into the clutches of the Spanish. The monarchs of both lands, priding themselves that they were loyal and influential Catholics, agreed to accept the judgment of the Holy See.

The reigning pontiff, Alexander VI (pope from 1492 to 1503), was of the notorious Spanish Borja (Borgia) family and could hardly have been expected to be totally impartial. Yet through the treaty drawn up at Tordesillas in June 1494, Portugal emerged with richer booty than Spain could have wished or Portugal may at first have realized.

By that treaty, the overseas world, known and yet to be known, was divided by an imaginary north-south line about 1,000 miles (by today's measurements) west of the Azores. All lands to the west of that line were to belong to Spain and Portugal was to claim lands to the east. Where in the Orient the extension of such a line might run would long remain a matter of dispute between the two contending lands. The intent was to give Spain undisputed claim to the Americas (not yet so named) and to Portugal, Africa and lands farther to the east. As it turned out, the imaginary line had cut off for Portugal the South American bulge which is now part of Brazil—a fact that suggests to some historians that King John of Portugal may have known exactly what he was getting and that some unusually close-mouthed Portuguese mariners had already landed there. With or without exploitable treasure, it could serve, as it often has since, as a most convenient landfall for any sailing ship bound for the South Sea, as the Pacific Ocean was then referred to.

To anyone living five centuries later, it seems preposterous that even a Vicar of Christ dared assume the right to sponsor a division of the oceans and lands of this earth between two clamorous European nations, no matter how devoutly Catholic they might be. Pope Alexander VI was cheerfully ignoring the possible claims of equally Catholic Genoese and Venetians, among whom were so many enterprising seafarers and who had previously had a near monopoly of European spice marts. He was also ignoring the French whose mariners were among the world's boldest, and the Dutch and English whose later apostasy could not yet provide excuse for exclusion. The natives of those far lands, of course, had no recognizable rights save that of conversion to the Catholic faith.

It was a treaty whose divisive heritage persists even into our own times.

5

Passage to India

With the little matter of spheres of influence settled to Portuguese satisfaction, the king set about seeing to it that Bartholomew Dias's achievement was followed up. The man chosen to lead this important undertaking was Vasco da Gama, an ambitious member of the minor gentry who was known for his courage in battles and, almost as important, his personal integrity.

Born in the little seaport town of Sines, da Gama, son of the civil governor, grew up associating with fisherfolk, learning the ways of the sea and of sailors. Beyond that, little is known of his youth but that it further justified his choice, at the age of thirty-six, as leader of the India voyage. He was already then an expert navigator, known for his courage, ambition, pride, and the kind of unwavering steadfastness he would need to see the voyage through to successful completion. He was also an aristocrat at heart who, when the time should come that rewards were due, would expect titles as well as fortunes. His distinction was that he would have earned them.

"In the name of God, Amen!" begins the unknown chronicler of this new undertaking, "In the year 1497, King Dom Manuel, the first of that name in Portugal, despatched four vessels to make discoveries and go in search of spices. Vasco da Gama was the Captain-major of these vessels; Paulo da Gama, his brother, commanded one of them, and Nicolau Coelho another. We left Restelo on Saturday, July 8, 1497."[1]

Accompanying the little fleet, but not destined for India, was another vessel captained by Bartholomew Dias, the first Portuguese mariner to sail around the tip of Africa. By 8 November, the fleet was casting anchor in St. Helen's Bay, on the west coast of Africa, a hundred or so miles to the north of the cape. There they remained "eight days, cleaning the ships, mending the sails and taking in wood." They must also have taken on the water, though it was not specifically mentioned.

Somewhere in the seas beyond the cape, they ran into storms so violent that the sailors, recalling the old tales of water pouring off the edge of the earth, threatened mutiny, begging the leader to head for hom before it was too late. Vasco da Gama firmly refused and the surviving ships continued north along the coast. After land encounters with a variety of peoples, both friendly and hostile, the little fleet dropped anchor finally, on 20 May 1498, at Calicut, after a voyage that had lasted eleven months.

The description of Calicut as first revealed to European eyes is both interesting and amusing, for the chronicler seems to have shared the illusion that all alien people who were not explicitly Moslem must be Christians. This was not too surprising for fifteenth-century men who had grown up in the Moslem-dominated Iberian Peninsula.

"When we arrived at Calecut," wrote the chronicler,

"they took us to a large church. . . . In the center of the body of the church rose a chapel, all built of hewn stone. . . . Within this sanctuary stood a small image which they said represented Our Lady. . . . Many other saints were painted on the walls of the church, wearing crowns. They were painted variously, with teeth protruding an inch from the mouth, and four or five arms."[2] It would take yet more voyages to teach the naïve Portuguese that this was no Christian church but a Hindu temple.

Fortunately for us, the goggle-eyed chronicler accompanied da Gama on his audience with the local king and left a record of his impressions.

> The king was in a small court, reclining upon a couch covered with a cloth of green velvet, above which was a good mattress, and upon this again a sheet of cotton stuff, very white and fine, more so than any linen. The cushions were after the same fashion. In his left hand the king held a very large golden cup [spittoon] having a capacity of half an almude [eight pints]. At its mouth this cup was two palmas [sixteen inches] wide, and apparently it was massive. Into this cup the king threw the husks of a certain herb which is chewed by the people of this country because of its soothing effect, and which they call *atambor* [betel-nut]. On the right side of the king stood a basin of gold, so large that a man might just encircle it with his arms; this contained the herbs. There were likewise many silver jugs. The canopy above the couch was all gilt.[3]

At the start, the king seemed friendly towards the strange visitors, but he was soon turned off by the gifts he was offered—ones better suited to savages, as the local Moslem merchants slyly pointed out. In early September, the Portuguese were glad to be able to depart

with their skins relatively intact. They managed, however, to load cargoes that would impress their own king
almost as much as the tales of massive gold bowls and
silver jugs.

The voyage home was stormy and difficult but by
the end of August 1499 the two surviving ships sailed
into Lisbon. For Vasco da Gama, it was a triumphal
return but for more than half of the men who had set
out with him two years before there was no return at all.
It is said that only fifty-five of the original complement
of 170 men were on the ships when they reached home.

Today a furious public outcry would follow the loss
of about two-thirds of the participants in a venture, but
in a time when wars, famine, and pestilence rode rough-
shod over all lands, such losses were more or less expected. The material returns were what counted and
even the small cargo of jewels and spices which the
Portuguese mariners had managed to acquire in India
was a dazzling revelation of the fortunes to be made
there. Stingy King Manuel was said to have realized a
sixtyfold profit on his investment in that voyage.

The king, who was on the point of marrying the
widowed daughter of Ferdinand and Isabella of Spain,
was soon writing them jubilantly about the return of
Vasco da Gama's ships:

> Most high and excellent Prince and Princess,
> most potent Lord and Lady: Your highnesses
> already know that we ordered Vasco da Gama,
> a nobleman of our household, and Paulo da
> Gama, his brother, to make discoveries by sea,
> and that two years have now gone by since their
> departure. And as the principal motive of this
> voyage has been, as with our predecessors, the
> service of God our Lord, and our own advan-
> tage, it pleased Him in his Mercy, to speed
> them on their way. From a message which has

now been brought to this city by one of the captains, we learn that they did reach and discover India, and other kingdoms and lordships bordering on it: that they entered and navigated its sea, finding large cities, large edifices and rivers, and great populations, among whom is carried on all the trade in spices and precious stones (which these explorers saw and met with in good numbers and of great size) which are forwarded to Mecca and thence to Cairo, whence they are dispersed throughout the world. Of these they have brought a quantity, including cinnamon, cloves, ginger, nutmeg, pepper, as well as other kinds, including the boughs and leaves of the same: also many fine stones of all sorts, such as rubies and others. And they also came to a country in which are mines of gold, of which, as well as of spices and precious stones they did not bring as much as they could have, for they took no merchandise with them that suited the market.[4]

King Manuel's twin motives—"the service of God our Lord" (of course as interpreted by him) and "our own advantage"—become even more evident as the letter continues:

As we are aware that your Hignesses will hear of these things with much pleasure and satisfaction, we thought it well to give this information. As your highnesses may believe, in accordance with what we have learnt concerning the Christian people whom these explorers reached, that it will be possible, notwithstanding that they are not as yet strong in the faith or possessed of a thorough knowledge of it, to do much in the service of God and the exalta-

tion of the Holy Faith, once they shall have
been converted and duly fortified in it. And
when they shall have thus been fortified in the
Faith there will be an opportunity for destroy-
ing the Moors of those parts. However, we
hope, with the help of God, that the great
trade which now enriches the Moors of those
parts, through whose hands it passes without
the intervention of other persons or peoples,
shall, in consequence or our regulations be
diverted to the natives and ships of our own
kingdom, so that henceforth all Christendom
in this part of Europe, shall be able, in a large
measure to provide itself with spices and precious stones. This, with the help of God, who
in His mercy thus ordained it, will cause our
designs and intentions to be pushed with more
ardor especially as respects the war upon the
Moors of the territories conquered by us in
these parts, which your Highnesses are so
firmly resolved upon, and in which we are
equally zealous.[5]

It had been his own mariners, as he gloatingly pointed
out, who had been able to bring home negotiable proof
that they had not only reached India, but had gathered
there spices and precious stones—something which Ferdinand and Isabella's navigator, Christopher Columbus,
had not done in those lands to the west. Neither sponsoring land could possibly foresee at the time all that
either achievement boded for the future. One thing that
was bound to follow for all European monarchs was an
accelerated interest in locating more sources of spices
and precious stones. Another, that was to cost them
dearly in lives and fortunes, was a growing determination
to neutralize in any way they could the dominant position of Moslem traders in the various courts of India.

Politics and religion handily joined forces in support of this determination.

For Vasco da Gama, the immediate result of his successful return was that he became a national hero. But a knightly hero of the fifteenth century was no legendary Sir Galahad. He was, of necessity, brave to the point of recklessness, if the situation demanded it. He gave unswerving devotion to king and Church—questioning the authority of either would have been nothing short of blasphemy—risking his person and fortune, if he had any, in their service. Their presumed enemies were to be slaughtered with great enthusiasm. If he happened to be fortunate enough to survive such encounters, he expected rewards both on earth and in heaven and was not backward in demanding them from the appropriate sources. In short, under a thin veneer of civilization, he was at heart an unregenerate savage.

While da Gama waited impatiently for the castles and titles he believed to be due him, King Manuel lost no time in consolidating the gains in the East. Within less than six months, another fleet had been fitted out for passage to India and on 9 March 1500 it set sail under the command of Pedro Alvares Cabral. More than a fleet commander, Cabral was being sent as official envoy of the monarch who had lost no time in styling himself, "King, by the Grace of God, of Portugal and of the Algarves, both on this side of the sea and beyond it in Africa, Lord of Guinea and of the Conquest, Navigation, and Commerce of Ethiopia, Arabia, Persia, and India." He did not include that Brazilian bulge on the South American continent though he may, even then, have been aware of Portugal's possible claims there. These would soon be made evident when, on 22 April 1500, Cabral's fleet (either by accident or design) stopped by a new land which they called *Terra da Santa Cruz* and which, as Brazil, was soon to serve as a convenient landfall for ships bound for Far Eastern seas.

Cabral's fleet numbered thirteen vessels, powerfully armed for those times. On one of these vessels was Bartholomew Dias whose discoveries and loyal service had again won him command. A month after the fleet left Brazil, a sudden tornado came up, scattering the ships. Four foundered with all hands on board, including Dias's caravel—thus consigning him to a grave in waters he had been the first to explore.

The remaining vessels of Cabral's fleet arrived off Calicut by the middle of September 1500. There they tried to establish a factory but soon got into trouble with the Moslem merchants who incited a mob to attack the factory and put its occupants to the sword. After bombarding the city in retaliation and thus setting it on fire, Cabral sailed on along the Malabar coast (the west coast of India) to Cochin, where he obtained permission from the local ruler to found a factory. Presently, on the Coromandel coast, on the east side of the Indian subcontinent, Cabral's ships were loading pepper for the homeward voyage. He delivered it in Lisbon on 31 July 1501. Barely six months were to pass after Cabral's return when Vasco da Gama, who had then become officially entitled to use the honorific "Dom" before his name, again set sail, this time with a fleet of fifteen ships under his command. Leaving in his wake the usual trail of blood and ashes, he reached Calicut by the end of October 1502. A typical episode had taken place when, approaching the Malabar coast, the fleet overtook a large dhow, the *Meri*, carrying Mohammedan pilgrims returning from Mecca. A seaman-chronicler tells that the dhow had enough wealth on board to "ransom every Christian slave in the kingdom of Fez." When the dhow's owners refused to hand over the wealth, the Portuguese took what they considered appropriate action. A second chronicler described it unemotionally: "We took a Mecca ship on board of which were 380 men and many women and children, and we took from it fully 12,000 ducats, with goods worth at least another 10,000. And so we burned the ship and all the people on board with gunpowder, on the first of October.''

Piracy, no less! Callous indifference to human life and to human suffering seem to have been as much a prerequisite for success in the Age of Exploration as was the greed for gold and jewels and, of course, for negotiable commodities and personal power. A man of compassion who rejected slavery and torture, those commonplaces of the sixteenth century, could hardly have risen to eminence in the Church itself. Bishop Torquemada, the Grand Inquisitor, suggests the kind of man then honored by churchmen as well as laity.

After arriving back in Lisbon on 1 September 1503, Dom Vasco went into a retirement that lasted twenty-one years. Married to a lady of rank, endowed with generous pensions which had the added virtue of being transferable to his heirs, he settled down to raise a family of six sons and one daughter, undoubtedly watching Far Eastern affairs with a critical eye. The consolidation of power on the Malabar coast was continuing under an able viceroy, Francisco de Almeida (1505–1509), and a still abler one, Alfonso de Albuquerque, whose period there (1509–1515) was marked by the conquest of Goa, about halfway up the Malabar coast, which would for centuries remain a center of Portuguese power in the East. Albuquerque died in Goa in 1515, but in the meantime he earned a name for integrity, for loyalty to his sovereign, and for the rough, sometimes savage justice by which he maintained and expanded Portuguese power and trade. Native Indians, rulers included, respected him highly.

Albuquerque's death in India—the life span of viceroys in the climate of India in those days was conspicuously short—was followed by a series of viceroys who felt their chief task to be the lining of their own pockets. Becoming aware of this, King Manuel's successor, John III, decided he must send a viceroy strong enough and honest enough to administer the colony as it should be administered. He chose Vasco da Gama, then an alert sixty-five. With fourteen ships under his command, Dom Vasco, together with sons Estevão and Paulo, sailed from Lisbon in April 1524.

This was a quite different passage to India than Dom Vasco's first when few believed that he could succeed in reaching his destination or, having reached it, return again to his native land. This time he surrounded himself with all the pomp and circumstance belonging to a Count of Vidigueira (a reward he had finally managed to extract from King Manuel), Admiral of the Indies, and Viceroy of India. The ceremony he maintained on board his flagship, *St. Catherine of Mt. Sinai*, suggests the value placed not only on the viceroy's person but also on the gold and spices India was already yielding to the Portuguese. A contemporary chronicler has left an impressive account.

> The said Dom Vasco brought with him great state, and was served by men bearing silver maces, by a major domo, and two pages with gold neck-chains, many equerries, and body servants, very well clothed and cared for; he also brought rich vessels of silver, and rich tapestry of Flanders, and for the table at which he sate brocade cloths. . . . He had a guard of two hundred men, with gilt pikes, clothed with his livery; all the gentlemen and honorable persons ate with him.[6]

All this pomp and circumstance, which surely delighted Dom Vasco's heart, could have compounded disaster had storms or hostile fleets met the ships at sea. Barring such possibilities—remote by Dom Vasco's expectations—the magnificence would serve to impress both the rulers they met along the way and those in India who had scorned the unsuitable gifts he had previously brought in the hopes of sweetening relations.

Dom Vasco had come a very long way indeed in the quarter-century since his last voyage. Luxury, however, had not spoiled the incorruptible hero. He set out immediately to reestablish discipline, which had become deplorably lax, and thus to put the king's affairs in order. His own affairs he could not long control for he had arrived an ailing man and, on Christmas Eve, 1524, a mere three months after reaching Goa, he died.

6

To Goa—and Back?

It was a tragedy for more than Dom Vasco and his family that he did not live to rule with his strong, if ruthless, hand. Had he lived and been succeeded by men of his ilk, it is hardly imaginable that the *Carreira da India*, as the regular sailing for India was called, could have so deteriorated that soon anyone setting out on it would have less than an even chance of surviving. However, set out they did; the chances for poor men to make fortunes there were too tempting and greed won the day. A series of accounts, originally published as pamphlets and later assembled under the title *Tragic History of the Sea*, picture some notably tragic Portuguese voyages, but only ones from which there were survivors to tell the tales of woe and chroniclers to record them. The period that *Tragic History* covers is from the mid-sixteenth century to the end of the first quarter of the seventeenth century when the growing interest of other European nations in the Far East began to add to the hazards already accepted as a part of the *Carreira da India*.

Those basic hazards originally had little to do with

international politics. Overloading and overcrowding, combined with a lack of even the most elementary hygiene, produced in the great carracks conditions it is very hard to believe. Some of the worst conditions might have been improved had not authorities in Portugal come to accept them as the expected price for reaching golden, spice-rich Goa. Homefront officials could hardly have long remained totally ignorant of or unmoved by such tales of filth, disease, and misery thaat would have trickled back to Portugal. An Italian priest, courageously undertaking the voyage in 1574, described the casual attitude of those embarking: "It is astounding to see the facility and frequence with which the Portuguese embark for India. . . . Each year four or five carracks leave Lisbon full of them, and they embark as if they were going no further than a league from Lisbon, taking with them only a shirt and two loaves of bread in the hand, and carrying a cheese and a jar of marmalade, without any other kind of provision." If they expected to be able to secure further provision from the carrack's stores, they were generally doomed to disappointment.

What were those vessels like in which sixteenth- and seventeenth-century Portuguese set sail for the ends of the earth? Large and imposing products of the ship-builder's art, those carracks dwarfed the caravels which boasted no more than 200 tuns burden (the English *Mayflower* of the same era was a mere 180 tuns). Provided with four masts, the foremast carrying a square sail while the other three were lateen-rigged, caravels were swift and maneuverable and were used more for carrying dispatches than for carrying cargoes and passengers. It was the great carracks that provided the romance as well as the tragedies of the *Carreira da India*.

We get a glimpse of such vessels through the observant and generally undazzled eyes of the Frenchman, François Pyrard de Laval, who was detained in Goa during the first decade of the seventeenth century.

First as to the Portuguese ships, in ordinary course three or four go out every year; these are the carracks, called by them *nãos de voyage,* which are sent out with the intention that they shall return if they can. . . .

These carracks are ordinarily of 1500 to 2000 tuns burthen, sometimes more, so that they are the largest vessels in the world, as far as I have been able to learn; they cannot float in less than ten fathoms [about 60 feet] of water. . . . These great carracks have four decks or stories, on each of which a man, however tall, can walk without touching his head against the deck above; indeed he comes not within two feet of it. The poop and prow are higher than the main deck by the height of three or even four men, in such wise that it seems as if two castles were erected at the two ends . . . the masts are so enormous that no tree is tall or thick enough to make a whole one—I speak both of the mainmast and the foremast. So, usually, all their masts are lengthened by splicing. . . . The yard is of thickness proportionate to the mast, and four-and-twenty fathoms in length [about 144 feet]. It requires full two hundred persons to raise it aloft, and always with two big capstans. . . .

These vessels go for trade, and never for war. The other, smaller ships, such as . . . caravels remain in the Indies to make voyages to China, Malaca, Mozambique, Ormuz, and other parts of India; but their chief use is that the King of Spain [at the time of Pyrard's writing, he was also the king of Portugal] sends them to accompany the carracks, and to convey men to the Indies; and if all the ships that go were to come back, there would not be found hands to man them, by reason of the great number that die on the voyages. Sometimes the hands of two ships are not sufficient to man one. Then, again, they obtain not enough cargo, that is, pepper, to fill them; and most often, for want of it, one or two of these carracks have to wait for the next year; and so, when the next year comes, they send out from Portugal only one or two carracks, supported by some smaller vessels.[1]

Should anyone stranded in Goa by this lack of larger vessels wish to return to Europe before conditions suited or authorities were ready to grant permission and offer passage, he had to buy a place for himself and for his "baggage and goods" at a high price. Pyrard wrote, "The condition of a man who has no berth on board is pitiful indeed: it is not as in our [French] vessels where the 'tween decks is common to all; in theirs there is not the smallest corner that is not given as a favor or sold, and the same on deck."[2]

Contrasting carracks and caravels, Pyrard wrote, "It is more honorable to be a mariner in the one than a mate in the other, wherefore a place in a carrack is sought after and purchased, being as well honorable as profitable." In most vessels, sailors were rough and violent men but the mariners in those carracks "are exceptions, for they are courteous and well mannered, both at sea and on shore, and seemed to be all men of honor and birth, bearing great respect to one another." This, however, did not keep them from putting on airs once their ship had safely passed the Cape of Good Hope and they had convinced themselves that Goa was practically within sight and that they should be received there as gentlemen from the homeland. There were generally, according to Pyrard, between 1000 and 1200 in a carrack's crew, never less than 800.

Particularly interesting is Pyrard's description of the duties of everyone from captain and pilot down to cabin boy. A sergeant who was "to execute the commands of the captain in matters of justice," was also assigned "charge of the fires, and no one, whoever he might be, would dare to light or carry any fire without the sergeant give it with his own hand. And for this purpose there are on the two sides of the ship at the place of the mainmast, two large kitchens"—clearly no more than two large sandboxes.[3] After giving account of the scanty provisions issued, Pyrard describes the use of such "kitchens":

> But the evil that I find in all this is, that the provisions are given to them raw, and each man has to cook his own victuals; so that you will sometimes see more than eighty or a hundred pots on the fire at the same time; and when some are done, others are put on. So when any are sick, instead of being properly cared for, they are exceeding ill fed and maintained, and many die from this cause. The French and Hollanders have not the same practice, for they have one cook for all, and eat six off a dish. . . .
>
> These ships are mighty foul, and stink withal; the most not troubling themselves to go on deck for their necessities, which is in part the cause that so many die. The Spaniards, French, and Italians do the same; but the English and Hollanders are exceeding scrupulous and cleanly.[4]

Ships sailed from Lisbon by the end of February under orders not to touch at any place before the cape "except in case of urgent need." On the far side of the cape, Mozambique was the only permitted harbor and then only for as brief a pause as possible. Nine or ten months might be consumed in the passage to Goa, the carrack by then usually grievously undermanned with its seamen hardly able to function at all. "While I was at Goa," Pyrard wrote, "I saw some ships arrive there, in which, of the thousand or twelve hundred men that were in them at the setting out from Lisbon, there were left not two hundred, and well nigh all these sick of scurvy, which wears them in such sort, that after they are arrived, they hardly recover."[5]

Pyrard had sailed from St. Malo in 1601 on one of the early French ships to undertake a voyage to the Far East. Since this was in direct challenge to Portuguese edicts that claimed all the East for its exclusive sphere of influence, the French were asking for trouble. They got it in several ways, the worst and last being to pile up on the Maldive Islands, to the southwest of India's southern tip. There the Portuguese found Pyrard and other survivors and took them as prisoners to Goa where Pyrard knew he must expect stern, possibly cruel imprisonment with little hope of ever again returning to Europe. Contrary to expectations and by reason of service in the Portuguese army in the East, Pyrard finally won his way to freedom and a return voyage. He credited his success in part to his skill in feigning stupidity while, incidentally, observing sharply and recording mentally fascinating details of life in contemporary Portuguese India. He knew that had the Portuguese authorities had any suspicion that the dumb soldier was eventually to publish his observations, they would have detained him in India for life, perhaps executing him on the spot.

At length, and undoubtedly with a great sigh of relief,

> arrived the time for our taking ship, which we did on the 30th January, 1610. We went on board by night on account of the tide; but this is a dangerous time by reason of the robbers then abroad who lie in wait for the poor folks

that are going aboard with their baggage and merchandise and rob and plunder them, nay, sometimes maim and murder them. . . .

It is a marvel to embark on one of these vessels that seem like castles, with the vast number of people on board and the merchandise they carry. Ours was so laden with goods on the deck that they reached almost half-way up the mast; and outside on the chain-wales, which are the ledges on each side, you saw nothing but merchandise, provisions, and bunks, which are the little cabins wherein the mariners and others lie, covering them over with fresh ox and cow hides. In short the whole place was so obstructed that one could hardly get about.[6]

The fortune seekers who took passage in such vessels should have known that they were not going on any carefree cruise for, even with all the losses at sea, enough men had returned to Lisbon to tell of their travels and an understanding of the risks were common currency in that port. Yet many Portuguese travellers seemed willing to accept the overcrowding, lack of hygiene, disease, storms, and even shipwrecks as the price of arriving within reach of the wealth of spice-rich India. The few berths that might have been allotted to officers or skilled seamen were generally sold by them to passengers, the sailors hopefully expecting to find somewhere, somehow a space to lie down in. In the tropical heat of the doldrums where a ship might lie becalmed for weeks, food grew rancid and whatever water remained on board became undrinkable. Scurvy raised its ugly head and was soon added to seasickness and dysentery, and these, with no one assigned the duty of cleaning up messes, presently made the carrack a floating pesthouse.

The grim situation on a carrack could become yet

grimmer as small differences between prickly *fidalgos* grew to explosive proportions. All too aware of this possibility, one governor of India commented acidly on the situation he had learned of in the carrack *Santo Espirito* after her arrival in Goa in 1546, that all the officers had mistresses and were at odds with the captain, and that it should be ordained that any master, pilot, or other ship's officer who brings out a mistress or takes one during the voyage should suffer capital punishment. The governor judged this to be the "principal cause of all the disasters and broils which occur in the carracks."

The pecking order on a carrack, as described in some detail by Pyrard de Laval, should be of considerable interest to a mariner of our own day: "There is a captain, who is absolute over the whole ship and the men on board; next there is a pilot, a second pilot, a master, a master's mate, a guardian, two ropemakers, some 60 mariners, 70 or more apprentices, and a master gunner."[7] Just where the remainder of that "more than 1000 or 1200, or at least 800 or 900" fit in the scheme of things is not quite clear. Certainly, with the anticipated losses along the way, many more than immediately needed had to be enrolled as replacements in various jobs.

"The captain has command over all, both the crew and the passengers, and for all they may be greater lords than he, yet they must obey him." Clearly a captain was expected to have and to exercise the authority to stop the "disasters and broils which occur in the carracks." Equally clear is that even when a captain himself avoided such broils, he could do little to anticipate and avoid them for others. One suspects that the captain himself might have had a mistress along.

It was the pilot to whom the nitty-gritty of ship management was entrusted: "After the captain, the pilot is the second person of the ship, for the master obeys him, and acts only under his commands." And the master "commands all the mariners, apprentices, and other ships' hands; he has a master's mate under him to assist him; all these are appointed by the king"[8] who might or might not be familiar with the daily problems of navigating a great top-heavy carrack from Lisbon to Goa. Certainly, an appointment coming from so high a source did little to enforce discipline or inspire good navigation in an incompetent appointee. If the pilot of the *Santo Espirito* was as lax as the other officers, the situation might have become grim indeed had that carrack been storm-buffeted to the point of foundering.

The statistics tell a tale of growing laxity. In the years between 1500 and 1580, thirty-one Indiamen were wrecked. In the following thirty years, the number of wrecked ships was thirty-five! Of the seventeen carracks that sailed from Lisbon from 1590 to 1592, only two returned in safety. An estimate puts the total loss in the 100 years after 1550 at about 130 carracks, with all the cargoes and most of the lives on board forfeited. Even without the grim wars to come, the estimated expenditure of "one thousand lives a cargo" would not be very wide of the mark.

It was not overcrowding but overloading that proved the greatest hazard of the return voyages. Holds were filled beyond capacity with bulky cargoes of pepper, cinnamon, and cloves when these became available in quantity. Here and there were stowed further items like saltpeter, indigo, locally carved furniture, and fine textiles of cotton and silk, cotton then being a rarity in Europe. Whatever could not be crowded into the hold filled every nook and cranny between and above decks. Here, too, officers and seamen sold space to the highest bidder, apparently believing that the kinds of disasters that had so frequently overtaken other overloaded hulks, couldn't happen to theirs.

Diego de Couto (1542–1616), one of whose distinctions was the ability to survive for fifty years in Goa, became official chronicler there and keeper of the records. In his usual frank and crusty manner he recorded an account given him of a typical disaster. Leaving Cochin—a second Portuguese enclave on the Malabar coast far to the south of Goa—in January 1589, the carrack *São Thomé* was leaking badly by the time she reached the vicinity of Madagascar, then called São Lourenço by the Portuguese:

> And this was due to the caulking, for which reason many ships are lost, which is very carelessly done, to which the officers pay little heed, as if so many lives and so many goods which are embarked in these great ships were not their responsibility. . . . All worked day and night at the pumps . . . without leaving them even to eat. . . . Yet notwithstanding all this diligence, the water gained ever more rapidly, so that they resolved to seek the nearest land and run the ship ashore there. They therefore put about under the foresail and the spritsail, not daring to set the mainsail, since they could not let go of the pumps . . . for any time that they did so would suffice to let them be submerged.
>
> While they were steering towards the land, it being already the 14th of March, the hold became waterlogged, and the pumps became blocked with pepper . . . so that they ceased to work.[9]

Somehow they managed to clear the once valuable pepper away but after two more days had passed, they launched the ship's boat and crowded her with many, but not all, of the people. No one was exercising authority. Soon it became evident the boat was overburdened and the officers "insisted that some persons should be thrown into the sea to save the rest. To this those gentlemen consented, leaving the selection of them to the officers, who at once threw six people into the sea. These were lifted up into the air and thrown overboard, where they were swallowed up by the cruel waves and never reappeared. This pitiful sacrifice so horrified those who witnessed it that they were in a daze, not realizing what they saw, or regarding it as something seen in a dream."[10]

Of the 104 people left in the boat, more were presently tossed overboard—much like cattle, it appears. The callous acceptance of the drowning of the people deserted on the ship as well as of those tossed into the sea now seems incredible but it can, perhaps, be explained by the fact that all the people involved expected they would receive their rewards in heaven. By 20 March, the survivors had landed somewhere along the Natal coast and started their approximately six-hundred-mile-long trek north to the Portuguese fortress at Sofala, relying for sustenance on land where natives might or might not feel friendly. The survivors reached Sofala in October 1589, and a year later were picked up by a Portuguese vessel.

In those days of sail, as one experienced navigator has noted, no one made a really good voyage without a certain amount of luck. But the *Carreira da India* relied too heavily on luck. With stricter ordinances or just the strict enforcement of ordinances already passed, there need not have been so many maritime tragedies. It was not only the *Carreira da India* but Portugal herself that was following a downward path. A small country with limited manpower, further limited by constant and foolish wars against the Moors, even after they had been pushed back into Africa, she could grow the crops her people needed only as her mariners brought back African slaves to cultivate them. Native-born Portuguese were being scattered far and wide, manning fortresses in Africa, Asia, and Brazil. Wars and sea tragedies continued to take their toll and as fewer desirables were left to call upon, the authorities emptied the jails for sailors to man the ships and the far fortresses.

In the last analysis, it was the corruption which the above situation led to that brought about the decline and fall of the Portuguese empire. There simply were not enough potential governors of the calibre of Almeida or Albuquerque or even of lesser men to fill the far greater number of less glamorous posts in the Far East. In an era when a man, no matter how skilled and knowledgeable, was nothing if he could not achieve the fortune of a millionaire or the status of a *fidalgo* (nobleman), the East, far from the observant eye of the government at home, could offer chances of quickly achieving both aims.

This situation developed over the years so gradually, perhaps, that most Portuguese were inclined to take it all for granted. But when a young foreigner found employment in Goa and undertook to record what he observed there, the whole sordid business came to light, thereby suggesting to heretic lands like England and the Netherlands that Portuguese India might be ripe for the picking.

Jan Huygen van Linschoten was born in 1563 in the Netherlands. Of an alert and adventurous turn of mind, at the age of seventeen he joined his two elder brothers in Lisbon, where they were merchants. None of the scant biographical sketches available suggest whether young Jan Huygen was a heretic or not. If he was, he concealed it well, for two years after reaching Lisbon, he joined the staff of the newly appointed Archbishop of Goa and set forth for the East where he would remain thirteen years. Like the Frenchman Pyrard de Laval, he observed much in Portuguese India and asked penetrating questions of people who had been able to reach points as far east as Japan. Like Pyrard, he made special note of the arrogance, greed, and corruption of the

Portuguese officials in Goa. When, in the mid-1590s, Jan Huygen was back in his homeland—and, incidentally, hobnobbing with a distinguished Dutch heretic—he wrote down an account of his stay in the East. This was promptly translated into English, so that both Dutch and English adventurers would have the benefit of those observations and could judge for themselves their prospects in the East.

"Everie 3 yeares," runs Linschoten's account, "there is a new Viceroy sent into India, and some time they stay longer, as it pleaseth the King, but verie few of them." As for the Viceroy, he "is very magnificent in his estate, and goeth little out, but sometimes on Sundaies, or holy daies, when hee goeth to Church, and when he goeth out of his house, the Trumpets and Shalmes do sound" (Shalmes being an antique kind of oboe). Accompanied by "all the Gentlemen and townes men of Goa, that have (or keepe) horses,"[11] the display was impressively magnificent, suggesting personal wealth acquired by the questionable means which the writer goes on to explain.

With some minor adjustments in punctuation and to help sort out just who was doing what, Linschoten's account continues:

> The Viceroyes, in the last yeare of their government, do use to visit the Forts lying round about the countrie, which is fiftie, sixtie, or eightie miles long, on the North and South side of Goa, to see how they are governed. They looke well unto them, but commonly an other supplyeth their place, and if they doe it themselves, it is more to fill their purses, and to get presents, than to further the commonwealth. These Viceroyes have great revenewes; they may spend, give, and keepe the Kings treasure, which is verie much, and doe with it what

pleaseth them, for it is their choyse, having full and absolute power from the king, in such sorte, that they gather and horde up a mightie quantitie of treasure, for that besides their great allowance from the King, they have great presents and giftes bestowed upon them. For it is the custome in those countries when any Viceroy commeth newly over, that all the native kings bordering on Goa, and that have peace and friendship with the Portingales, do then send their Ambassadours unto him, to confirme their leagues with great and rich presents, therewith likewise to bid the Viceroy welcome, which amounteth to a great masse of treasure. . . .

When the Viceroy has continued out his time and when an other Viceroy arriveth in the countrie, he does presently dispatch his Lieuetenant, with full power and authoritie in the name of his maister, to receive possession of the government of India, and prepare the Palace for him, for there stayeth not a stoole or bench within the house, nor one pennie in the treasure, but the house is left as bare and naked as possible so that the new Viceroy must make provision for to furnish it and gather new treasure. In the same shippe wherein the new Viceroy commeth thether, the old returneth home.

Because their time of government is so short, and that the place is given them in recompence of their service, and thereafter not to serve any more, there is not one of them that esteemeth the profit of the commonwealth, or the furtherance of the Kings service, but rather their own particular commodities, as you may verie well thinke, so that the common speech in India is, that they never looke for

any profit or furtherance of the common wealth
by any Viceroy, as long as the government of
three yeares is not altered. For they say, it is
bound to be most true, that the first yeare of
the Viceroyes time, he hath enough to do to
repaire and furnish his house, and to know the
manners and customes of the countries, without any further troubling of himselfe. The
seconde yeare to gather treasure, and to look
unto his particular profits, for which he came
into India. The third and last yeare to prepare
himselfe and set al things in order, that he be
not overtaken or surprised by the new Viceroy
when he commeth, but that he may returne
into Portingall with the goods which he had
scraped together. The same is to bee under-
stoode of all the Captaines in the Fortes and of
all other officers in India. Wherefore it is to be
considered, how they use themselves in their
places and the Kings service, whereof the inhabitants and married Portingales doe continually speake, but they are farre from the Kings
hearing, who knoweth not but that his officers
doe him good service, whereby there is small
remedie or amendment to be hoped for.[12]

All this might be ascribed to the natural prejudice of a
Dutchman against any rule emanating from the Iberian
Peninsula which had for so long held the Netherlands in
merciless subjection. But the same picture was drawn,
using almost the same phrases, by the unquestionably
Catholic Frenchman, Francois Pyrard de Laval, not too
many years after Linschoten. Pyrard depicts the same
decadence, the same arrogance of corrupt and grasping
administrators. It was no mere coincidence that the
English were to found their East India Company in
1600, with the Dutch East India Company following just

two years later. The never very influential French East India Company was not to appear for some decades.

It would not have taken a moralist to foresee retribution. Any sober, realistic politician should have been able to recognize that Portugal's world empire was already doomed. The situation had been grim enough while Portugal had no need to contest Far Eastern power with European rivals and while her own kings had some understanding of and concern for their far-flung empire—concern, that is, beyond the acquisition of treasure. But when the rules of royal succession put a fourteen-year-old incompetent on the throne—Sebastián I, whose reign, 1557 to 1578, was dedicated to his personal crusade against the infidel and whose land eventually, for lack of more immediate heirs, would come under his uncle Philip II of Spain as Philip I of Portugal—the cracks in the structure of the Portuguese empire began to widen. A ruler as obsessed as had been Sebastián with a mission to spread Christianity and destroy heresy, heretic-baiter Philip looked with disfavor on the Dutch ships that had been picking up oriental commodities in Lisbon for distribution to other ports of Europe. When finally in 1598, Philip formally decreed that no such heretic ships should have access to Lisbon, Dutch navigators were ready and waiting for the signal to undertake their own trading voyages directly to the East.

A nineteenth-century historian summed it all up effectively: "It may well be asked whether Portugal would not be happier now, and richer, too, had she never had the opportunity of dwelling on those ancient glories; had the wealth of the Indies never been poured into her lap, only to breed corruption; had her strength not been wasted in a struggle to which she was materially unequal, and which ended in exhaustion and ruin."[13] Curiously, that Portuguese-Christian enclave, Goa, with its magnificent churches conjuring up dimming memories of a great lost empire, hung on until 1961 as a Portuguese possession where Portugal had long been functioning rather as custodian of some ancient monument than as administrator of an integral part of modern India.

7

So Noble a Captain

Despite mounting maritime losses, enormous fortunes continued to be reaped in the spice trade. Such successes strengthened the Portuguese conviction that the sea route which Vasco da Gama had scouted out must remain a Portuguese monopoly. To assure this, fortresses had been built and manned at strategic points along the route. Armed vessels equipped to fight off all challengers—or so the Portuguese believed—were kept at sea.

Wishful thinking led the Portuguese king, Manuel I, to believe that Vasco da Gama had discovered the one and only possible route to the East. Taking no chances, however, after Pedro Alvares Cabral stumbled on Brazil in 1500, Manuel sent out two expeditions in 1501 and 1503 to further explore the coast on which it was found and to determine exactly which new lands might belong to Portugal by virtue of the treaty drawn up at Tordesillas. Even more important loomed the question as to whether the newly discovered land might be crossed by a navigable passage to the South Sea, as the Pacific was then referred to. The pilot of these expeditions was a clever Portuguese named Gonzalo Coelho, but the member to win enduring fame was a voluble, conceited Florentine, Amerigo Vespucci, whose boastings convinced the Portuguese of his great navigational skill and whose name undeservedly would become attached to the newly discovered continent.

These expeditions of 1501 and 1503 convinced Manuel that there was no possible sea passage across this land mass. He could see no value in spending any more of the wealth accruing to him from Far Eastern commodities on seeking a westward route to the Orient. Ironically, he repeated the mistake of his predecessor, King John, who had rejected Columbus, with similar consequences—leaving a determined, ambitious mariner free to seek sponsorship at the Spanish court.

This time the man thus snubbed by the Portuguese king was no foreigner, as the Genoese navigator had been, but a born and bred son of Portugal, Fernão de Magalhães. Magalhães was to become, in Spain, Fernando, or Hernando Magallanes and to go down in American history as Ferdinand Magellan. Born about 1480, of a noble family in one of Portugal's rugged northernmost provinces, Magellan had influential relatives who helped place him, while yet a teenager, as a page in the household of King John's queen, Leonor. When King John died in 1495, Magellan was transferred to the household of his successor, Manuel, and was later permitted to volunteer for service in India under the first Portuguese viceroy, the distinguished and incorruptible Dom Francisco de Almeida.

Sailing from Lisbon in 1505, Magellan reached the East via the usual Portuguese route, served there for the next six years, and became involved in several military engagements. In one of these he received a wound which left him with a permanent limp. Back in Portugal as a veteran soldier and a sailor who had mastered the art and science of navigation, Magellan was already obsessed with the idea of finding a route to the west and thus materially shortening the distance to be navigated to reach the East. Why he believed there was a navigable passage across the continent that barred the way is not clear. It may simply have been that the coastline of South America was known to slant in toward the west.

While developing his plans and waiting for a suitable opportunity to seek the sponsorship of the king, Magellan served briefly as a soldier in Morocco during one of Portugal's never-ending encounters with the Moors. In 1517, Magellan had his audience with Manuel who, it was said, always loathed him, although no contemporary chronicler explained exactly why this was so. Later Portuguese made the ex post facto suggestion that it was because Magellan sold his rejected services to a rival king. Yet such peddling of services among European courts was accepted with other navigators like the Italians Christopher Columbus and Giovanni Caboto, each of whom tried his luck in four different courts.

For the Portuguese, Magellan's special sin was that he had the right idea and that for a second time, through his action, a Portuguese monarch was to be outdone by a Spanish rival. Though of a noble family, Magellan was no courtier's courtier, but a man of action whose qualities of person and spirit contrasted strikingly with the kind of men a king usually surrounded himself with. So strong was Manuel's aversion to this particular courtier that he is said to have curtly denied him permission to kiss the royal hand in farewell. The implication was that it was of no interest to his king where Magellan might choose to sell his services. It became a matter of great interest to later Portuguese. Like Columbus, Magellan offered his services to the king of Spain, Charles I, who as Charles V of Burgundy was shortly to become Holy Roman Emperor.

What was Magellan, this would-be explorer of a new

ocean route to the East, like? How did he impress men
of his own time? The mutinous captains who sailed
under Magellan were known to hate the Portuguese
interloper and might be expected to do everything in
their power to discredit him and exalt themselves. A
worshipful young Italian volunteer, on the other hand,
saw him as "so noble a captain." Fortunately, we have a
more impartial record left by a man who had no personal
reason either to praise or to blame. This was Bartolomé
de Las Casas, Bishop of Chiapas, then a northern prov-
ince of Guatemala but now part of Mexico. As son and
nephew of men who had accompanied Columbus on his
second voyage, Las Casas was well aware of the personal
qualities needed by an explorer setting forth to face
unknown dangers. As a religious well known for his
active denunciation of fellow Spaniards' exploitation of
American natives, Las Casas was not a man to conceal
any disparaging thoughts he may have had about Magellan.

It was late in the year 1517 when the interview
described by Las Casas took place:

> At this time there cam to Valladolid in flight (or
> at least secretly, because of some grudge his
> king held) a mariner (or at least a man who
> knew much of the sea) called Hernando Magal-
> lanes, which is Magalhães in Portuguese, and
> with him a student (or who, at least, claimed
> to be a student) named Ruy Faleiro, pretending
> to be a great astrologer; but the Portuguese
> insisted he was possessed by a demon and
> really knew nothing of astrology as he claimed.
> These two offered to show that the Isles of
> Maluco, from which the Portuguese carried
> spices to Portugal, lay within the line of demar-
> cation drawn between the King of Castile and
> Dom João of Portugal . . . and that they would

discover a way to go thither outside of the way
taken by the Portuguese, and this would be a
certain strait of which they knew. With this
new idea, they came first to the Bishop of
Burgos, since they knew that until then he had
governed the Indies . . . and the Bishop took
them to the Grand Chancellor and the Grand
Chancellor talked to the king. . . . Magellan
brought with him a well painted globe showing
all the lands, and on it he pointed out the way
he proposed to follow, except for the strait
which was not shown so that no one should
anticipate him. And on that day I happened to
be in the chamber of the Grand Chancellor
when the bishop brought him in and he showed
the Grand Chancellor the route he intended to
follow; and when I talked with Magellan, asking, "What route do you plan to take?" he
replied he wished to go by the Cape of Santa
María, which we call the Rio de la Plata, and
thence follow along the coast until reaching the
strait. I further asked him, "And if you find no
strait by which to pass to the other sea?" He
replied, "And if no strait is found, I'll take the
Portuguese route." But according to a letter
written by an Italian gentleman named Pigafetta, of Vicenza, who was with Magellan on
that voyage, Magellan felt certain of finding the
strait, because he told of having seen on a map
made by the great cosmographer, Martin of
Bohemia, that was in the treasury of the King
of Portugal, the strait drawn in the manner he
described. And because that strait was situated
among lands situated within the limits claimed
by the Castilian monarchs, he felt obliged to
offer himself to the King of Castile to discover

this new route to the Isles of Maluco and others.[1]

Just six years Magellan's senior, Las Casas was well equipped to pass judgment on his venturesome contemporary in a way men of our own century are not: "This Hernando de Magallanes had to be a man of spirit and of brave ideas for undertaking untried things, although his person did not suggest great authority since he was of small stature and did not look like much, so that people thought that they could easily impose on and deceive him."[2] People were to learn the hard way that this man of modest appearance and small stature, exaggerated by his limping gait, had a large endowment of the qualities required to be the leader of a long voyage to an uncertain destination—courage and decisiveness among them.

Magellan reached Seville and won the attention of men of importance, including a highly prosperous fellow expatriate from Portugal, Diego Barbosa. Barbosa's son Duarte volunteered for Magellan's proposed voyage and his daughter Beatriz was given in marriage to Magellan with her brother's hearty approval. Diego Barbosa was unable to finance the proposed expedition himself, but he used his influence at court in Magellan's behalf. By March 1518, articles of agreement between Magellan and the Spanish king had been drawn up and duly signed.

All this time, spies were busily sending reports to the Portuguese monarch. Manuel regretted his foolishness in letting Magellan leave Portugal when he could have detained him indefinitely. He strove to remedy his mistake by subterfuge. Convinced that Magellan's proposed expedition would menace the spice monopoly of the Portuguese empire, Manuel sent a special secret agent, Sebastian Alvares, to spy on Magellan and to arrange, if possible, that nothing should come of Magellan's grand design.

By July 1518, Alvares had sent lengthy reports to his royal master. He described Magellan's ships, their personnel, armaments, victualing, and any other details he was able to ferret out through the sly questioning for which he seemed to have a special talent. He even had the effrontery to visit Magellan, appealing to the captain's loyalty to the land of his birth and promising advancement should he cancel his agreement with the Spanish.

"I will," Alvares assured the king, "watch the service of Your Highness to the full extent of my power."[3] This "full extent" might have included arrangements for the elimination of Magellan should all other schemes fail. Alvares may have doubted, however, that this would achieve his sovereign's aims. He wrote, "It seems to me that if Fernan Magellan were removed, that Ruy Faleiro would follow whatever Magellan did." Thus Magellan's death would be of no help where the main object of the Portuguese monarch was to prevent the sailing of a Spanish-sponsored expedition under *any* captain. Alvares assured his employer piously, "Please God the Almighty, that they make such a voyage as did the Cortereals!"—that is, never be heard of again—"and that your Highness may be at rest, and ever envied, as you are, by all princes!"[4] To this end the king's secret agent endeavored to ensure the failure of the Spanish expedition by subverting ships' suppliers and captains.

Magellan, being a man of his land and times had, even before being subjected to Alvares's hypocritical blandishments, harbored some suspicions about the kind of schemes the spy might be setting afoot. Yet, unshaken in his determination and devout in his faith in God, he went purposefully ahead with his preparations. While the ships, under his ever-watchful eye, were being readied for the long and challenging voyage, he struggled to enroll able men to sail under his leadership. Their number has been variously estimated as 237 or 277, many of them Spanish nationals, as the agreement with King Charles had specified. Thirty-seven were Portuguese, but they could not be counted on for loyalty since some were likely in Manuel's pay and others might be subvertible by Alvares.

As it turned out, a very important member of the expedition was neither Spanish nor Portuguese, but an Italian gentleman-volunteer, young Antonio Pigafetta of Vicenza, who left for posterity the only detailed eye witness account of Magellan's voyage. "Prompted by a craving for experience and glory,"[5] he had persuaded the Spanish king as well as the papal ambassador, in whose suite he had arrived in Seville in May 1519, to allow him to volunteer for the voyage. Thus Pigafetta was able to take part in last minute preparations as well as in the solemn ceremony performed immediately before departure in the chapel of Santa María de la Victoria in Triana, Seville. At this ceremony, he saw Magellan presented with a royal standard and heard all the men who were to sail swear to obey Magellan in everything.

On 10 August 1519, Magellan's fleet of five vessels—the flagship or "capitana" *Trinidad,* and ships *Victoria, Concepción, Santiago,* and *San Antonio*—left Seville, dropped down the river Guadalquivir to Sanlúcar de Barrameda, and anchored under the castle from which, almost seventy years later, a reluctant Duke of Medina Sidonia would be summoned by King Charles's son, Philip II to take command of the Spanish Armada. It took several days for the fleet to reach that anchorage and about a month more before it was ready to make a final departure. Already Magellan began to uncover the treachery of the landsharks who, undoubtedly encouraged, if not bribed by Alvares, had supplied putrid meat, weevily biscuits, and everything in short weight. All such supplies had to be replaced by fresh ones brought down

river from Seville on slow barges. Even so, the extent of
the cheating was not fully apparent until the fleet had
settled in at its wintering harbor in Patagonia.

Well before they reached Patagonia, however, Magellan had faced graver handicaps of a human kind.
Magellan knew how to deal with common seamen. In
the remote Portuguese coastal town where he grew up
his only playmates must have been the sons of sailors
and of fisherfolk. Thus, it was not the sailors but the
officers of his fleet who made it plain that the cards had
been stacked against him. No sixteenth-century captain
was completely free to select his officers with an eye
exclusively to their personal merits, martial qualities,
seamanship, and above all, their capacity for loyalty.
Like other European lands, Spain was full of poor and
petty nobles who, as younger sons, were cut off from an
inheritance. They had to fight their way upward with
their wits and, often, without regard to conscience. So
much, then, for the solemn vows they had taken in the
chapel of Santa María de la Victoria.

Even more burdensome to Magellan must have been
the royal and ecclesiastical bastards whose influential
fathers did not hesitate to force their sons on voyages
that could earn them fortunes which might be useful in
purchasing titles or legitimizing their status. Whatever
their lack of qualifications, they could not be excluded
from a voyage that promised fabulous rewards in oriental
commodities.

As a special misfortune, Magellan had to deal with
Juan de Fonseca, Bishop of Burgos, who held by royal
appointment an influential post in the Casa de Contra-
tación that controlled overseas affairs. Since he had no
interest in the exploration of new routes, the bishop had
done his best—or perhaps his worst—to guard the Casa'a
funds by hampering the efforts of Columbus, Balboa
and Cortéz. Since Magellan's voyage, sponsored by the
king himself, seemed inevitable, Fonseca saw in it an

opportunity to advance the fortunes of his bastard, Juan de Cartagena, as captain of the *San Antonio;* of his favorite, Luís de Mendoza, as captain of the *Victoria;* and of his special servant, Gaspar de Quesada, as captain of the *Concepción*. None of these three had had any maritime experience or boasted any navigational skills. Furthermore, they vied with one another by bringing large retinues of pages and servants on the voyage. These contributed nothing but hearty appetites that would aggravate the starvation soon to be faced by everyone in the fleet. As was the custom, pilots of inferior social status were put in charge of the actual navigation. Thus, Magellan could only rely on the loyalty of Juan Serrão, captain of the little *Santiago,* like his leader a voluntary exile from Portugal. He was the brother of Magellan's good friend Francisco Serrão, whom Magellan hoped to meet once more in the East. When the crunch finally came, only Juan Serrão joined Magellan in facing down the other captains whose hostility grew as the voyage progressed.

At Tenerife, an urgent message from his father-in-law caught up with Magellan, warning him that his three Spanish captains were plotting to kill him. Pigafetta recorded his awareness of the menacing situation with the added personal comment, "I don't know why they hated him, except that he was Portuguese and they Spaniards."[6] This suggests that Pigafetta had not observed Magellan in any of the wanton acts of cruelty that Spanish survivors of the expedition were eventually to ascribe to the captain.

Further information gleaned during the call at Tenerife alerted Magellan to the not-too-surprising fact that the king of Portugal had sent out a fleet to intercept his Atlantic crossing. Knowing this, Magellan wisely avoided the usual transatlantic routes to keep south along the African coast until he could make a shorter and less frequented crossing to the bulge of Brazil in the vicinity of today's Pernambuco. In taking this route, the fleet became caught in the equatorial doldrums in whose oppressive heat they lay becalmed for many days. This did nothing to improve the dispositions or loyalty of the prickly Spanish captains who were planning and staging their first attempt at inciting mutiny.

Because of the Portuguese threat, Magellan made no stop in Pernambuco but coasted south to spend Christmas near today's Rio de Janeiro. Here again mutiny threatened and this time Magellan controlled it with the local assistance of fresh food and the compliant females of the Indian natives. The day after Christmas the fleet left all these delights behind, to the increased grumbling of captains and crews. Heading south, again close to the coast, they explored every bay and inlet for the hoped-for passage to the South Sea.

By 31 March, with the equinox past, they reached Port San Julian which was situated, as Magellan was presently to learn, less than 200 miles north of the entrance to the desired passage. Perceiving that the far southern winter was closing in, Magellan decided to remain until spring in the unprepossessing harbor. The land was bleak, the climate grim, and time lay heavy on the hands of men who undoubtedly had set forth with assurances that they would not be too harshly judged should they succeed with mutiny—including liquidation of the captain—and then take the whole fleet back to Spain.

Here Magellan's qualities of great leadership showed themselves. He managed to quell the mutiny promptly, condemning to the gallows ringleaders Captains Mendoza and Quesada. The other mutineer was Bishop Fonseca's "nephew," Juan de Cartagena, who was, however, spared the indignity of having his body left swaying in the Patagonian wind. He was condemned to be left behind in Patagonia after the fleet had departed, in company with an equally mutinous priest.

Magellan could not afford to liquidate all whom he knew to have contemplated mutiny, for there were no replacements closer than Spain for their navigational skills. He pardoned two who were possessed of such skills, clearly hoping that the fate of their fellow conspirators might have a sobering effect. These two were the *Concepción*'s master (that is, pilot), the Portuguese João Lopes de Carvalho, who had been one of the first to pilot a Portuguese fleet to Brazil, and the same ship's Spanish assistant master, Juan Sebastián Elcano, an able and ambitious navigator who, ironically, would surely have been ignored by history had he succeeded in his scheme by taking the fleet directly back to Spain. As it turned out, fate and Spanish nationalism combined to lay on his disloyal head the laurels that should have been Magellan's.

During the four-month San Julián interlude, the little seventy-five-tun *Santiago*, under the loyal captain Serrão, kept busy trying to explore the coastline toward the south. It was wrecked there; crew, supplies, and most of the caravel's gear were salvaged and distributed among the four remaining ships. By August all the vessels were again heading south. Two months later, and almost by accident, they sailed into an inlet which turned out to be the entrance to that winding, 350-mile-long strait that now bears Magellan's name. At about this point, the *San Antonio* deserted to head back for Spain via Port San Julián where it picked up the mutinous captain and priest Magellan had left marooned there. These two added their complaints and accusations to those the officers and crew of the *San Antonio* were planning to register against their Portuguese captain-general.

The remaining three ships kept on through the tortuous, stormy strait, to emerge thirty-eight days later in the limitless ocean which Magellan then found so peaceful that he misnamed it "Pacific." It was a moment of triumph, but those who thought they were leaving behind all their troubles for a swift crossing of a narrow ocean were soon to be bitterly disillusioned.

Pigafetta recorded, "On Wednesday, 28th November, we left the strait and entered the ocean to which afterwards we gave the denomination Pacific, and in which we sailed for the space of three months and twenty days without taking any fresh provisions. The biscuits we were eating no longer deserved the name of bread; it was nothing but dust, and worms which consumed the substance; and what is more, it smelled intolerably, being impregnated with the urine of mice. The water which we were obliged to drink was equally putrid and offensive. We were even so far reduced, that we might not die of hunger, to eat pieces of leather with which the main-yard was covered to prevent it from wearing the rope. Sawdust was also eaten as well as mice which, when caught, could be sold for half a ducat apiece."[7] Half a ducat of gold!

On 24 January 1521, two months after emerging from the strait, the starving men were tantalized by the sighting of a wooded islet, now thought to have been Pukapuka, but it was uninhabited and, much worse, could offer no "practicable anchorage." Eleven days later they sighted another such island, probably today's Caroline, that proved to be equally devoid of anchorage. Soundings have since revealed that the sea bottom nearest to Pukapuka is 2010 meters (6595 feet) deep and for Caroline, 1370 meters (5106 feet)—hardly places where any vessel, let alone a sixteenth-century sailing ship, could hope for an anchor to hold. The starving fleet had to sail on.

For the men, the worst torment was neither hunger nor thirst, but that dreaded accompaniment of long voyages, scurvy. "The gums of both the lower and upper teeth of some of our men swelled so that they could not eat under any circumstances," Pigafetta reported. Subcutaneous hemorrhages, such as those which blackened swollen gums, also affected body joints, making the sufferer unable to perform shipboard tasks. As on all such voyages, many people died, mostly of scurvy, every day their bodies being thrown into the sea three or four at a time.

Centuries after Magellan's voyage, scurvy was still an expected, if not understood, risk of every long voyage as it was, incidentally, of every winterbound frontier community in our own land. If people in such communities were lucky, they might have knowledgeable Indian neighbors who could effect miraculous cures with preparations of spruce beer. No one had the slightest idea what the curative element in spruce beer might be. It was not until the twentieth century that antiscorbutic vitamin C in greens and fresh fruits as well as in the inner bark of spruce trees was recognized as the preventative of scurvy.

Remedies were already on hand in the sixteenth century had they been recognized as such. Both Magellan and Pigafetta escaped scurvy and doubtless ascribed it to the vigilance of a protective deity. Neither would have credited their good fortune to the quince jelly which Magellan had along as a delicacy to relieve the monotonous and unappetizing diet he knew he must be subjected to. We can imagine him sharing this luxury with the young Italian volunteer, Pigafetta.

On 6 March 1521, and nearly 100 days' sailing from the strait, the ships sighted two lofty islands where anchoring was possible. These islands, now known as Guam and Rota, were almost at once called "Los Ladrones" because of the natives' propensity for swarming over the ships to take off with every movable article to be found on them. Hastily acquiring a supply of rice, fruits, and water, Magellan left the islands after three days. About ten days later they reached the island group to be known as the Philippines in honor of the future

Philip II of Spain. At the time of Magellan's arrival, these islands were not known to any Europeans, so to him goes the credit for discovery.

Here, at Cebu, approximately two weeks later, Magellan sponsored the conversion to his own faith of the local Rajah and about 800 of his subjects. Then he made an unsolicited offer to help this newly Christianized Rajah overcome a neighboring pagan ruler. Typically, Europeans who for the first time encountered the dazzling lifestyles of native rulers liked to dazzle in return by demonstrating military might which relied upon steel armor and an arsenal of weapons. In undertaking such a battle, Magellan made his greatest and final mistake.

Pigafetta described the fight, in which he personally took part, in some detail, notably the climax when Magellan, trying to hold off enemy pursuit while his companions made their way back to the ships, received fatal wounds. "Thus," wrote the young Italian, "they killed our mirror, our light, our comfort and our true guide. When they wounded him, he turned back many times to see whether we were all in the boats. Then, seeing him dead, we wounded made the best of our way to the boats, which were already pulling away. Except for him, not one of the boats would have been saved, for while he was fighting, the rest retired."[8] It was not a very gallant performance, but perhaps understandable if any wished to survive to tell the tale.

Magellan's own log and journal never reached Spain. It seems likely that they were deliberately destroyed by his successor as captain-general of the expedition, one of the previously mutinous captains who wished that no records should remain to embarrass him and his co-conspirators. Others suggest that finally, on the voyage home, it was the Portuguese who seized and destroyed those records when the single remaining ship, *Trinidad*, put in at the Cape Verde Islands. In any case, none of Magellan's own records have survived to speak for him.

Speaking eloquently for the lost leader was again young Pigafetta: "Among other virtues which he possessed, he was always the most constant in greatest adversity. He endured hunger better than all the rest, and, more accurately than any man in the world, he understood dead reckoning and celestial navigation. And that this was the truth appeared evident, since no other had so much talent, nor the ardor to learn how to go around the world, as he almost did."[9]

8

The World Encircled

Though not large in terms of the number of men lost, the losses at Cebu were very great in terms of leadership. By local treachery, as well as in the fight itself, many of the fleet's most able navigators were lost, including those most devoted to Magellan. Among those were Captain Juan Serrão, as well as Magellan's illegitimate son, Cristobal Rebelo, and his brother-in-law, Duarte Barbosa.

Juan de Carvalho immediately thrust himself into the leadership void, assuming the position of captain-general. If Pigafetta was privy to them, he carefully avoided recording the discussions among the surviving officers as they hurriedly made preparations to depart from Cebu which, incidentally, soon relapsed into paganism. Home must then have looked infinitely desirable to men who had suffered so much, but to go home now without accomplishing the great purpose of locating a new route to an eastern empire was taking a grave chance. There might be an accounting, too, for the dark crime of mutiny, despite all efforts to destroy the evidence. They might fare considerably better and possibly even enrich themselves should they first find some spices and fill their ships' holds before returning.

A plan of action had to be worked out and this was done in a gathering of officers who began by endorsing Carvalho's elevation to the captain-generalship. They then faced further grave decisions. With only about 110 men remaining of those originally sailing from Spain, there were not enough sailors to man the three remaining ships. Of these, *Concepción*, her planks riddled with teredo worms, had to be scrapped. Her hull was burned to the water's edge. Her erstwhile master, Elcano, became captain of the *Victoria*. For months the two surviving vessels cruised around, performing profitable little acts of piracy.

Even by the most direct route, the way home was thousands of miles and many months long even had the two ships headed directly for Spain. But the Spice Islands had been the goal set by the Spanish king and six months were spent in rather aimless cruising while Captain Carvalho acquired for himself a harem of Moslem beauties. He must surely have taken special delight that he was no longer under the strictures imposed by Magellan who always stoutly refused to permit women to sail on his ships. Stopping to rob native vessels they encountered, Carvalho shanghaied the native pilots in hopes of finding a guide to the Spice Islands. They finally reached them in November 1521, under the guidance of the one kidnapped pilot who had not managed to jump overboard and swim ashore.

It would be interesting to learn just how Pigafetta, who had been so conspicuously devoted to Magellan, managed to survive while keeping a journal that was hardly flattering to his present superiors. Could it be that none of those officers suspected that he kept a journal? Could they have discounted its importance? Or was it simply that there was no one on board literate enough to read Pigafetta's Italian? Perhaps, well aware of the undercurrent of treachery, Pigafetta had been wise enough to make himself both as inconspicuous and as helpful as possible, performing for his promised, not overgenerous, salary of 1,000 maravedis a month, whatever tasks might be assigned him. Europeans were in increasingly short supply on the ships, native sailors having been enrolled (or shanghaied) as replacements for those who had died. The survival of Pigafetta's journal may have been thanks to the fact that the mere business of keeping the ship afloat and on course absorbed all attention.

When the *Trinidad* and the *Victoria* reached their destination, as Pigafetta reported: "The pilot who still remained with us told us that these four islands were Maluco,"—the Moluccas, or Spice Islands—"so that we thanked God and for joy discharged all our artillery. And no wonder we were so joyful, for we had spent twenty-seven months less two days in our search for Molucca."[1]

A couple of days later the two ships entered the harbor and anchored off the most important island of the group, Tidore. It was actually quite small in area, no more than ten miles in length. Of the other four islands, circular Ternate was only six miles in diameter. It is very hard to believe that these mere specks on the surface of a great ocean could have produced the means of supporting their own rulers in imposing state, of luring so many sixteenth-century mariners to their doom, and of being the root cause of so many grim struggles between remote nations of Europe who were eager to gain control of their spice riches.

Trinidad and *Victoria* passed six idyllic weeks in the islands while the men refreshed themselves and traded for the cargoes that were to justify all past expenditures in men and money. The sultan welcomed them cordially and arranged to have a shelter built near the shore to protect the ships' merchandise. Though the sultan may not have known it, much of this had been won by piracy from native junks.

While watching and recording, Pigafetta did a bit of trading on his own. "Thither we carried all we had to barter, and placed it in the custody of three of our men. For ten ells of red cloth of pretty good quantity"—an ell being somewhat under a yard—"they gave a bahar [about 400 pounds] of cloves, for fifteen hatchets a bahar, for thirty-five glass cups a bahar; and the king in this manner had from us almost all our goblets. . . . Many of the above-mentioned goods had been obtained by us by the capture of the junks, which I have related; and the haste we were in to return to Spain caused us to sell our goods at a lower price than we should have done, had we not been in a hurry."[2]

Pigafetta, at least, was not so preoccupied with a return home that he did not investigate the reason for being there—the spice trees:

> The same day I went ashore to see how the cloves grow and this is what I observed. The tree from which they are gathered is high, and its trunk is as thick as a man's body, more or less, according to the age of the plant. Its branches spread out somewhat in the middle of the tree, but near the top they form a pyramid. The bark is of an olive color, and the leaves very like those of laurel. The cloves grow at the end of little branches in bunches of ten or twenty . . . are white when they first sprout, they get red as they ripen, and blacken when dry. . . . The leaf, the bark, and the wood, as long as they are green, have the strength and fragrance of the fruit itself. . . .
>
> There are in this island of Giailolo some trees of nutmegs. These are like our walnuts, and the leaves are also similar. The nutmeg,

when gathered, is like the quince in form and color, and the down which covers it, but it is smaller. The outside rind is as thick as the green rind of our walnuts, beneath which is a thin web, or rather cartilage, under which is the mace, of a very bright red, which covers and surrounds the rind of the nuts, inside which is the nutmeg properly so called.

They also grow in Tadore the ginger. . . . Ginger is not a tree, but a shrub, which sends out of the earth shoots a span long like the shoots of canes, which they resemble in the shape of the leaves, only those of ginger are narrower . . . that which makes the ginger is the root.[3]

Of cinnamon, Pigafetta wrote, "It is a small tree not more than three or four cubits [five to six feet] high and of the thickness of a man's finger, and it has not got more than three or four little branches. The leaf is like that of the laurel. The cinnamon for use which comes to us, is its bark, which is gathered twice a year."[4] Incidentally, the only spice found in the Philippine Islands, as Magellan discovered, was cinnamon, though in quite limited quantity.

Pigafetta and his shipmates busily purchased the valuable spices with whatever personal articles they could spare for barter. Soon the holds of both ships were so overcrowded with the spice cargo that the *Trinidad*, the original fleet's *capitana*, burst her seams and started leaking so badly that she had to be careened. This meant running her up on the beach, unloading her cargo, repairing the leaks, then reloading her cargo. It was a process that consumed over three months, during which period Carvalho died and was replaced by Captain Gomez de Espinosa, whose loyalty to Magellan at San Julian had helped save the voyage.

Meanwhile, on 21 December 1521, *Victoria* under Elcano set sail for Spain with only forty-seven of her original crew and thirteen native seamen. It was agreed that *Trinidad*, when made seaworthy once more, should head for Nueva España and send her cargo across to the Caribbean to be reshipped to Spain. Thus, it was thought, they were ensuring that at least one ship should arrive in Seville with the great news of the newfound passage and the coveted cargo.

For the *Trinidad*, laden with nearly fifty tons of cloves, the attempt to negotiate an eastward passage proved disastrous. Months later, with thirty of her crew of fifty-three dead of scurvy and others disabled by that disease, she limped back to Tidore. There the Portuguese, who had been scouring the seas to intercept Magellan, picked up the ship, stripped her and let her drag ashore to end up a total loss. As for the remaining Spaniards on the *Trinidad*, the Portuguese officer cynically reported to his king that he had detained them in Maluco because it was an unhealthy country, "with the intention of having them die there." Only four lived to reach Spain again years later. Having survived the rigors of voyaging and imprisonment with hard labor by the Portuguese in the East, they were promptly rewarded with Spanish imprisonment after reaching their native land.

Thus, Captain Elcano was the only one of all the men of Magellan's fleet to receive glory or material reward for the venture. The ex-mutineer captain reached Spain in August 1522 after a harrowing nine-month voyage, to be received with noisy acclaim. There returned with him no more than eighteen survivors out of the over 250 people who had set out—a record to rival any of the Portuguese voyages described in the *Tragic History of the Sea*. The important fact was that they had actually completed the first world-encircling voyage, having added a new archipelago to the empire claimed by the Spanish king. Moreover, they brought with them a spice cargo valuable enough to cover several times over the money expended for the voyage.

In September, Elcano made his report to the then-King, Charles: "Most high and illustrious majesty: Your high majesty will learn how we eighteen men only have returned with one of the five ships which Your Majesty sent to discover the Spicery with Captain Ferdinand Magellan (to whom glory); and so that Your Majesty may have news of the principal things which we have passed through, I write and say briefly this." Briefly, as promised, he describes the finding of and passing through the Strait and the crossing of the Pacific to an "archipelago of many islands quite abundant in gold. We lost by his death the said Captain Ferdinand Magellan, with many others, and unable to sail for want of people, very few having survived, we dismantled one of the ships and with the two remaining sailed from island to island, seeking how to arrive, with God's grace, at the Isles of Maluco, which we did eight months after the death of the said Captain, and there we loaded the two ships with spicery. Your Majesty should know how, navigating towards the said Isles of Maluco, we found cloves, cinnamon and pearls."[5]

Elcano goes on to describe their discovery that one of the ships had become unseaworthy, adding piously that

> we resolved either to die, or honorably serve Your Majesty by informing him of the said discovery, to depart with one ship only, and she in such a bad state, because of the teredos, which only God knows; on this course we discovered many very rich islands, among them Banda, where ginger and nutmeg grow, and Zabba, where pepper grows, and Timor, where sandalwood grows, and in all the aforesaid is-

lands there is an infinite amount of ginger. The proof of all these productions, gathered in the same islands in which they grow, we bring to display to Your Majesty.

The treaties of peace and amity of all the kings and lords of said islands, signed by their own hands, we bring to Your Majesty, for they desire to serve you and obey you as their king and natural sovereign.[6]

The desires of the "kings and lords of said islands" would have been of only passing interest. What counted was that the desired direct access to the lands of pepper, ginger, nutmeg, and cloves had been achieved. The promise of future spice fortunes was what really mattered to King Charles. Losses in ships and human lives, as well as any questionable happenings along the way, were quite incidental. Thus Elcano, the Spanish ex-mutineer, was exalted, rewarded with the promise of a generous pension and also with a coat of arms which, among other items, displayed two crossed cinnamon sticks, three nutmegs and twelve cloves! The Portuguese Magellan's great and unique achievement, since there was no Spaniard to speak for him and since another man had brought home the spices, was not only ignored, but he was personally reviled.

With heady acclaim ringing in his ears and the promise of a royal pension, Elcano settled down to enjoy life in high style. His will listed newly purchased personal items like six pairs of shoes, nineteen shirts, jerkins, jackets, hats, caps, and such. Further, he acquired a mistress in Valladolid and another in San Sebastián. His two-timing soon involved him in the expense of a bodyguard to protect him from the furious relatives of one of the ladies. Meanwhile, to be on the safe side, he extracted a royal pardon not only for whatever part he had played in the San Julian mutiny but also for having,

on a previous voyage, sold a government ship. Enbol-
dened by success, Elcano demanded still more rewards,
among them the captain-generalcy of a new expedition
to the Spice Islands, command of a fortress to be built
there, support for various of his needy relations, and
election to the order of Santiago. But by this time,
Charles had had enough. Elcano had to remain content
with what he already had and this, incidentally, did not
include an installment of his pension during his lifetime.

For Magellan's achievements there was no recognition at all and no payment of any of the pension promised his family. His wife and children were soon dead
and none remained to plead his cause save the Italian
gentleman-volunteer whose voice was drowned in the
greedy clamor of envious, hostile men.

9

Route of the Manila Galleons

It may be that King Charles simply had a lapse of memory, forgetting all he had agreed upon at the time Magellan was organizing his voyage. It may equally well have been that by the time the remnant of Magellan's fleet returned to Seville, finding the far southern strait did not seem quite so important as it had a few years before. Across the Sea of Darkness had dawned a newer golden land—Mexico—where Spanish conquistadores were undertaking a venture that would make the old struggle with Portugal for access to the South Sea superfluous.

A scant four months before Magellan set sail, Hernando Cortéz and his small group of companions in arms landed on Mexican soil—a fact which could hardly, at the time of Magellan's sailing, have reached the royal ears. Cortéz went commissioned by Diego Velasquez, governor of Fernandina, as Cuba was then called, to seek out a presumably lost captain named Grijalva. Most important, he was to spy out the land for possibly valuable commodities. Velasquez's commission to Cortéz dwells on the need for gentle dealings with the natives to whom no Spaniard had, as yet, given sound reason for trust. Clearly, it would not be to Cortéz's or other Spaniards' advantage to add to the Spanish reputation for cruelty and deception. The Indians were to be taught to recognize the Spanish king in matters temporal and the Spanish God in matters spiritual.

Equally predictable were the closing items of Velasquez's thirty sections. Section 25 runs in part: "You are to make inquiry as to the things, both moral and material, of the lands you penetrate; whether there may be pearls, spices, gold, &c. particularly in Sta. María de las Nieves [Yucatan] whence Grijalva has sent me some grains of gold to have assayed." Section 26 reveals a credulity the sixteenth century had not yet outgrown: "Make special enquiry as to the kinds of people, for it is said there may be people with long, wide ears and others with faces like dogs, and where the Amazons dwell." Section 29 caps it all: "On arriving at Sta. María de las Nieves, send me in the ship which you can best spare whatever you may have secured by barter, samples of gold, pearls, spices, animals, birds, etc. encountered."[1]

Cortéz's undertaking was to succeed far beyond what the jealous, ambitious Velasquez expected or, for that matter, actually desired. Cortéz's glory was to far outshine that of the governor of Cuba, especially when the king began to receive his royal fifth of Mexico's treasures. It would be a while yet before the king came to appreciate the extra bonus of the long coastline presented by Mexico to the great South Sea, still more time before his mariners discovered a route by which the coastline could be reached from the Far East. In typically royal fashion, the king who had forgotten his commitment to Magellan eventually ignored his great debt to Hernando Cortéz. He did not forget that his realms had been enlarged to include a remote archipelago that was to give him access to the silks, spices, and other valuable products of long-fabled lands.

Precisely where in that ill-defined and remote Far East the archipelago was located, no one was able to tell then nor for two and a half centuries thereafter—not, in fact, until accurate chronometers (ships' clocks) made it possible to determine ships' longitudes with some degree of accuracy. It was all a matter of guess and dead reckoning for navigators of the sixteenth century, who also had to estimate the probable width of the Pacific Ocean, its currents, and its prevailing winds.

Despite such limitations, of which navigators became increasingly aware with experience, there were plenty of aspirants eager to be put in charge of a new expedition. Some may have been ignorant of the kind of ordeal they were so anxious to become involved in, but even experienced mariner Juan Sebastián Elcano, who already had learned the score the hard way, was ready to take part in another such venture. Elcano as Commander just might have brought it off, but he was forced to content himself with an appointment as chief pilot and second-in-command while the coveted plum dropped into the lap of a man whom Elcano obsequiously referred to as, *"Muy magnifico Señor Commendador Loyasa."*

An expedition under the leadership of Loyasa, whose chief qualifications for the position lay in the fact that he could claim close relationship with two bishops, was a total failure. Not even a single ship out of Loyasa's original fleet of seven survived to reach Spain again. Three ships were lost even before starting west through the straits. Of the remaining four, one caravel disappeared somewhere in the Pacific and another came to grief near the Spice Islands. The seventy-tun pinnace *Santiago* became separated from her sister ships and after a fifty-day-long voyage, arrived at Tehuantepec on Mexico's west coast in too bad condition to put to sea again. Thus alerted to the expedition's plight, Cortéz sent three rescue ships, of which two simply disappeared in the immenseness of the Pacific. The survivor, the *Florida*, reached what remained of the Loyasa expedition, but after two futile attempts to return east across the Pacific, had to be abandoned.

The usual physical sufferings of a long sea voyage had not spared this Pacific crossing of Loyasa's fleet. The captain-general died on 26 July 1526, to be followed two weeks later by his second in command. By then there were only 116 men alive on board—so barely alive that the young page, Andrés de Urdaneta recorded, "The people were so worn out from much work at the pumps, the violence of the sea, the insufficiency of food and illness, that some died every day."[2] After cruising aimlessly and searching in vain for Cipango (Japan) and its rich merchandise, or at the very least a haven and some supplies, they had a final encounter with the Portuguese. In January 1527, the one remaining ship of Loyasa's original fleet, the 300-tun capitana, *Santa Maria del la Victoria*, suffered badly in a naval encounter with the Portuguese at Tidore. Apparently as much because of vibrations from the discharge of her own guns as from the Portuguese shot, her seams opened and she could not be repaired without a prolonged beaching which the Portuguese presence made impossible. Her remaining crew set fire to the ship and burned her to the water's edge rather than have her taken over by the enemy.

The survivors shifted as best they could on shore. The weakened men felt obligated to follow their king's original instructions and to hold for him and Spain as much of the Spice Islands as possible. For these men, this meant fighting off the Portuguese they encountered, trying to enforce the claims against the far more numerous Portuguese who were bound to overcome them eventually. It must be said, however, that they enjoyed the local fruits, acquired local mistresses, and hunted to secure meat. Still, these lonely survivors must also have secretly questioned whether these lovely islands could really be worth their cost.

Meanwhile, the Spanish monarch, though apparently caring little about the physical sufferings of the men he had sacrificed, must have begun to ask himself whether the possession of that little group of remote Spice Islands in the Pacific could be worth all the money being expended in making good his claim to them. Undoubtedly, Charles's misgivings were reinforced by the fact that he was courting the Princess Ysabel of Portugal and thus in no position to contest possession of the Moluccas with her relatives. It was late December 1530 when the castaways in the Spice Islands received, via a newly arrived Portuguese governor, stunning news that put an end to all their efforts. The nearly bankrupt King Charles had officially renounced all claims to the Moluccas in favor of Portugal for the sum of 350,000 gold ducats, approximately one million dollars in terms of today's values. This would eventually be paid through indirect importation of spices from the islands.

The king was neatly getting something for nothing, since enforcing his claim to the Spice Islands was proving all but impossible. But for the barely twenty Spaniards remaining on Gilolo, it was a rude shock to learn that those who had already given their lives, "counting it an honor to die in the service of Your Majesty," had died in vain. Whatever had been decided in Europe, the survivors were still bound to the East with no way of sailing home, for their king had not seen himself as obligated to arrange that they be returned. A year later, as Urdaneta told it, they suffered great hardship as they were without shoes, had no money, and their own articles of barter had long since given out. The king of Gilolo was tired of providing for them for so long, and they had to revert entirely to the basic native life of gathering fruits and hunting game—no easy task while walking barefoot over sharp volcanic rocks or through coarse tropical grasses. After an eleven-year absence, seven men of the fleet's original total of 450 reached Spain again. Survivor Andrés de Urdaneta made an official report upon his repatriation in 1537. Whatever slightly seditious thoughts may have been raised in the minds of those neglected mariners by their king's renunciation of the Moluccas, they were as nothing compared to the reactions of merchants and mariners in Spain, who soon perceived that the king had sold them out. One merchant insisted that the emperor would have done better to pledge Estremadura, Serena or any other great cities and territories [of Spain] than Malacca, Sumatra, and the Moluccas. Some distraught merchants offered to raise personally the cash for paying off Charles's debt, if they could be reimbursed by being allowed, for a period of three years only, all the profit accruing to the Spanish spice trade. The imperial answer was that, "they should not . . . speak to him any more of this matter; whereat some marvelled, others were sorry, and all held their peace."

Charles, however, was in no way giving up his claims to the Philippines which, though producing negligible spice crops, might serve not only as spice entrepôts but also as intermediary centers for transshipment of silks, porcelains, and precious metals from China and Japan, if and when they located it. With the Mexican Pacific coast now available, Charles believed that he could send galleons from there on round trips to distant island possessions, transship their valuable return cargoes by mule and man across Mexico or Panama, and receive them in Spain, without Portuguese intervention. East coast ports like Veracruz or Nombre de Diós in Panama, would be used. The emperor still had to learn that though the Far East could be reached by sailing west from those Mexican Pacific ports, the return voyage east remained highly uncertain. The little *Florida*, sent to aid Loyasa's fleet, had twice tried to return that way, and given up after ocean winds and currents prevented passage. Unless and until such a passage could be made, a Manila galleon would have to take the long and hazardous voyage home through waters still dominated by unfriendly Portuguese.

No Spaniard in authority seems to have thought of giving up the dream of a sea route back and forth between Mexico's west coast and the Philippine Islands. No longer expecting to oust the Portuguese from the Spice Islands, the emperor and his advisers now hoped to use Manila as a depot in the new China trade, while possibly securing spices from the Moluccas by indirect means.

Although five east-west ventures had failed to complete the return trip, the emperor held to his conviction that one of his navigators must bring it off. When, in 1556, Charles abdicated in favor of his son Philip, it did not mean that there was to be a less stubborn Spanish monarch on the throne. Philip was as convinced as his father had been of a Spanish king's destiny to succeed in whatever venture he chose to sponsor. In 1560, success meant navigating the sea route he had decided upon. Believing firmly that God must be on his side, Philip had to recognize that God had not willed the previous attempts at a return Pacific crossing to succeed.

Clearly, to assist God, there must be on board more than a bishop's bastard or two. A skilled and knowledgeable navigator with some experience of Far Eastern matters, political and maritime, was needed. The emperor now fixed his hopes on the right man—the Basque Andrés de Urdaneta who, at the age of seventeen, had served as page and reporter on Loyasa's tragic voyage.

Urdaneta had learned a great deal about Far Eastern waters both by navigating small vessels there and by discussing larger problems of Pacific navigation with experienced seamen, both native and European. Men who knew the young Basque assured Philip that if anyone could succeed in finding the desired route, it would be this talented Urdaneta. There was, however, an obstacle which the devout Philip could not ignore. Some years before, at age forty-four, Urdaneta had forsworn the life of great activity in Mexico—first as army officer, then as corregidor and visitador—for the contemplative life of an Augustinian friar. Urdaneta truly believed himself finished with the layman's life, but Philip II, King of Spain and Holy Roman Emperor, thought otherwise and when he chose to express his thought, even a friar must find it an all-but-irresistible command.

In September 1560, Urdaneta received a letter dated April 1559 which ran: *"Devoto Fray Andrés de Urdaneta* of the Order of St. Augustine: I have been informed that, when a layman, you went in the armada of Loiasa passing the Straits of Magellan to the Spiceries, where you remained eight years in our service. And as now we have charged D. Luis de Velasco, our Viceroy of this New Spain, with sending two ships to discover the Isles of the West *(Poniente)* towards the Malucos . . . and because of the great knowledge you have of the affairs of that land, you being well acquainted with navigation there, as well as a fine cosmographer, it would be of great value if you went in said ships, both for the aforementioned navigation and for the service of the Lord, our God and for our own . . . I, the King."[3]

This was no mere sugggestion; it was as near a command as pious Philip would presume to issue to a friar. Urdaneta, possibly cherishing a secret yearning for the seafaring life, replied promptly. He would of course undertake the proposed voyage provided he could receive the consent of the father provincial of his order and the latter, Urdaneta was presently reporting to his "Sacred Catholic Royal Majesty," "has directed me to take part in the voyage with three other religious. And although I am now more than fifty-two years old and in poor health, owing to the hard labors in which I have been involved since my youth, the short remainder of my life was to have been spent in quiet, nevertheless, recognizing the great zeal of Your Majesty in all that pertains to the service of Our Lord and for the spread of the Holy Catholic Faith, I am now prepared to face the labors of this undertaking, trusting solely in Divine aid and hoping that Your Divine Majesty and Royal Person will be well served in this. . . ."[4]

Though the king's summons made clear that he wanted Urdaneta's well known skills for taking charge of this new venture, the friar could not, as a religious, accept an official appointment as captain-general of the fleet. Viceroy Don Luís de Velasco got around this difficulty for the king by letting Urdaneta suggest a nominal leader. This was Miguel Lópes de Legaspí, a fellow Basque of about Urdaneta's age, who understood the situation and accepted it. By 21 November 1564, Legaspí's fleet had been constructed, equipped, and made ready to sail from the port of Navidad. It consisted of two three-master galleons (the capitana *San Pedro*, 500 tuns, and the *San Pablo*, 300 tuns), two pinnaces (the *San Juan*, about 80 tuns, and the *San Lucas*, about 40 tuns), and a small frigate. On 23 January 1565, after two months at sea, the fleet reached Guam and about three weeks after that the Philippines. There they did their best to build the desired good relations with the native population, pardoning the slaughter of Magellan and his comrades.

What really mattered on this voyage was neither the route to the East in a westerly direction nor the winning of friends after reaching their destination, but a way back across the Pacific. Urdaneta, whose previous experience in the East warned him that the season to attempt such a passage would soon be past, lost no time in completing preparations for the return voyage. Again with a nominal captain—this time Legaspí's seventeen-year-old grandson—and with Urdaneta in actual charge, the *San Pablo* set sail by 1 June when, he believed, he might take advantage of the summer westerlies said to prevail in the northern Pacific at that season. It was no easy voyage, but by 18 September, they sighted an island off the California coast, since identified as near Santa Barbara. From there they coasted south, pausing only briefly at Navidad and ending the voyage at Urdaneta's preferred port, Acapulco, on 8 October 1565, four months and ten days after setting sail from the Philippines.

It was a triumph of discipline and skill—this route which started in a northerly direction then crossed the Pacific, taking advantage of winds and currents to reach the California shores. Urdaneta presently sent a brief and modest report: "We suffered much hardship on the voyage through bad weather and illness. Sixteen men died before reaching port, and four others died after arriving, also a native from the Ladrones, sent by the General with three other natives from Cebu."[5]

As always in such voyages, scurvy had been the great killer. Of the 195 men who survived to set foot in Acapulco, not more than eighteen were fit to work. Yet to seafarers of those times, the loss of a mere twenty men out of an initial number of about 215 was phenomenally low for any long ocean voyage.

Philip II was bound to see a route eastward across the Pacific as more than just an interesting achievement in seamanship. It enabled him to decree, with some likelihood of success, colonization of the Philippine Islands which he so wanted to believe were his. Never having doubted that the misplaced generosity of Pope Alexander VI gave Spain full claim to the archipelago which Magellan had first discovered a half-century earlier, Philip felt himself finally in a position to exploit that claim. This could be achieved only when Spaniards had settled in the islands. Though royal decrees might force Spaniards to sail to the East, it took other kinds of persuasion to keep them there. The climate of the Philippines might be just as unhealthy as in other Eastern lands. Social attractions in so small and remote a land would be very limited for Spaniards settling there. The praiseworthy winning of new souls to the Church was a project assumed by the religious who went out with the first ships and whose numbers increased with each later ship's arrival from the West. For the laity, compensations for life in distant, fever-ridden outposts like the Philippines had to be material so that people who went there might look forward to returning home wealthy, envied, and perhaps, with luck, ennobled.

Unlike Goa, Manila had few local products which might enrich the transplanted Spaniards called Manileños. There was some gold and silver, though far less than Mexico and Peru were pouring into royal Spanish coffers. There was a bit of cinnamon, but not of a quality or quantity to rival that which Ceylon was producing for the Portuguese. Much later there would be valuable products of the land, most notable of which was abaca of which exceptionally fine and strong ropes could be spun. But in the sixteenth and seventeenth centuries, the chief source of wealth was to be through acting as middlemen in the China trade with possibly some Japanese goods added for good measure.

The seamen who crossed the Pacific with government support—and few went without such backing—were always directed to report on the trade potential of any land they might reach. Thus, at Cebu in July 1567, Miguel López de Legaspí, who had been the commander of the fleet in which Urdaneta had sailed from Mexico, wrote Philip II that to the northwest were some large islands called Luzon and "Mindoro" to which Chinese and Japanese came yearly to sell silks, webbed stuffs, bells, porcelains, aromatics, tin, printed cotton cloths, and other such goods.[6]

Five years later, the English merchant, Henrie Hawkes, reported to Richard Hakluyt on trade between "New Spain" [Mexico] and the "Islands of China" [Philippines]: "They have in this port of Navidad, ordinarily their ships, which goe to the Islands of China, which are certain Islands, which they have found within these 7 yeeres. They have brought from thence gold, and much Cinamon, and dishes of earth, and cups of the same, so fine, that every man that may have a peece of them, will give the weight of silver for it. . . . Many things they bring from thence most excellent. There are many of these Islands, & the Spaniards have not many of them as yet: for the Portingals disturbe them much, & combate with them every day, saying it is part of their conquest. . . . The men of the maine lande, have certaine traffike with some of these Islanders, & come thither, in a kinde of ships, which they have with one saile, and bring of such merchandise as they have neede of. . . . And there is no doubt that the trade will be marvelous rich in time to come."[7]

The vehicle for such "marvelous rich trade" for nearly two and a half centuries was the yearly Manila galleon which the king in distant Seville subsidized and over every detail of whose functioning, as well as over the people of Manila, he and his council of the Indies kept jealous watch. This worked, as it rarely could have among heretic English colonists, because no yearning for liberty of person or conscience had motivated these Spanish settlers. Conceiving their empire to encompass the half of the globe not assigned to Portugal, neither Philip nor his Portuguese opposite number knew to whom the Philippine Islands really should belong. Although the Portuguese were periodically, and not always pacifically, to claim the islands, Manila's main problems were not caused by Portuguese interlopers but by the Spanish settlers. Friars, merchants, adventurers, and soldiers, many of whom the viceroy of Mexico had sent out in the hope that they would not return to trouble him, were the colonists of the Philippines. A far from harmonious lot, in Manila they all agreed upon one thing—

their right to share in the wealth which personal investment in the yearly galleon sailing might bring them.

Unlike the carracks that had long been plying between the Malabar coast of India and Portugal, the
galleons were not ships that reached the Far East already
half, if not totally worn out. They were constructed at
royal expense in the islands, Cavite in Manila Bay being
a place where many galleons were built and repaired
with native materials and by native workmen. The tropical hardwoods used for frame, sheathing, and planking
were strong and, even more important, practically proof
against the teredo worm. Chinese and Malay workmen
were generally highly skilled. Rigging ropes were spun
from fibers of the native banana-like plant, abaca, which
eventually was to reign supreme on the great sailing
ships of the world. Thus the East was able to produce
ships that could endure the heat, storms, and calms
through which they must sail. With all the local materials
and labor, one would not have expected the ships to be
as costly as they turned out to be for the royal exchequer.

Since the Manila galleons were intended primarily
for trade, their lading was very important and cargo space
at a premium for the Manileños. They were the king's
ships and the king in far away Seville had ordained to
whom and how cargo space should be allotted. All
citizens were to receive a share "in proportion to their
wealth" in order to join in the advantage and profit of
the traffic. The advantage for the king was that such
sharing might make residence in Manila look more attractive to those isolated colonists.

Within a long list of typically detailed Spanish regulations, there was no mention of space to be allowed for
piled up deck cargo such as had brought disaster to more
than one Portuguese carrack sailing from Goa round the
Cape of Good Hope. Unlike those Portuguese cargoes,
spices played a relatively minor role in those of the
galleons. Peppercorns were not to clog the pumps of

these ships. Here silks were the biggest, most profitable item, silken threads as well as many kinds of silken fabrics which had reached the Philippines from China.

Antonio de Morga, a high Spanish official serving in the islands from 1595 to 1603, gave a fascinating, lengthy description of the China-Philippine trade, offering a list of items that runs to over a crowded printed page: "A considerable number of *somas* and junks (which are large ships) come as a rule laden with goods from Great China to Manila. Every year thirty, sometimes forty, of these ships come . . . with the monsoon and in settled weather, which ordinarily comes with the March new moon. . . . They make the journey to Manila in fifteen or twenty days, sell their merchandise and return in good time, before the strong south-westerly winds set in at the end of May, or the first days of June, so as not to run into danger on their voyage."[8]

Launching into his list of ladings, Morga dwells especially on textiles, largely silks, ranging from raw unspun fibers to elaborately woven and embroidered damasks, but not overlooking other kinds of fibers from cottons to what may be the "grass linens" we associate with that part of the world. The list also includes porcelains, jewelry, furniture, fruits, ending with "pepper and other spices; and rarities, to recount all of which would mean never finishing, nor would even masses of paper suffice for the task."

Having gained official admittance to the port of Manila, the Chinese, who are referred to as "Sangleyes," started selling their wares to canny Manileños, some of whom may have kept a little for personal use but most of whom planned to send them on to Acapulco where such luxury goods usually brought high prices. "Likewise," Morga notes, "some Japanese and Portuguese merchant ships come annually,"[9] and again he lists the wares they may have brought to sell as well as those that have come from Borneo, mostly for sale to Philippine natives. The return cargo from Acapulco would be largely silver coin or bullion realized from the sale of the outward cargo and destined to purchase more goods from the Chinese.

After the trading junks had left Manila, little time remained before the Manileños had to have their bales of merchandise ready for the annual galleon sailing, unless they decided to await the following year's. Some years there were up to four galleons sailing in company, more often no more than two, and sometimes a single galleon fared forth to face the long tempestuous voyage along the route laid down by Friar Andrés de Urdaneta.

Inevitably, suggestions would be made to the conservative authorities about how that passage might be improved. These were apt first to focus on ways to get free from the tortuous passage through the archipelago, a journey that might consume several weeks. Then came the question of the best spot for turning sharply east, the place on the American coast to aim for, and how close to that coast it was desirable to sail. Generally about half a year was consumed in the eastward passage. A ship sailing by the end of June could not hope to drop anchor off Acapulco much before Christmas, though it might be still later or, in several notable instances, never. Small wonder that officers, passengers, and crew that had survived a stormy, scurvy-ridden passage expected to reimburse themselves generously by the sale of the goods which had accompanied them from Manila. The return voyage westward with prevailing winds and currents allowing passage in a more or less straight line consumed at least half the time of the outward passage.

For those on the receiving end of the cargoes in New Spain, there were high expectations of profits. As soon as a galleon had been sighted somewhere along Mexico's northwest coast a courier set forth posthaste for the capital to alert the Viceroy. This official would then prepare the usual proclamation of the opening of the fair in Acapulco, holding this proclamation until he had news that the galleon had actually reached port. Already, however, people had been galvanized into motion and thousands were soon converging on the grubby little port, converting it into what an Italian globetrotter of the eighteenth century considered a populous city. Once the goods had been landed and duly passed by customs officials who might, incidentally, demand their personal pound of flesh, bargaining over wares began and millions in silver changed hands. As the galleon made ready for the return voyage, the wares which had been sold made their difficult way by muleback along the nearly 300-mile-long "China Road"—really scarcely more than a rough track through wild country between the seaport and the high capital, where they could be resold at considerable profit.

Though heretic foreigners were, by edict, to have been totally excluded from Spanish overseas dominions, there were always some who managed to get in, possibly because such foreigners, having persuaded the authorities that they were practicing Catholics, managed to be profitable. They contributed toward spreading the word that millions of pesos were represented in the galleons' cargoes, suggesting to some of Spain's enemies that here was an opportunity not to be lost. Friar Andrés de Urdaneta had unwittingly contributed to this promotion.

As Urdaneta returned to conventual life, he prepared a chart showing "winds, promontories and capes" as well as ocean currents to be encountered on the route. Copies of this chart served as guides to future pilots who would follow that route each year, beginning in 1572 with the annual Manila galleons. It would also guide pirates and others who found the galleons irresistibly attractive.

Fourteen years after Urdaneta's voyage, that Spanish-baiting Englishman, Francis Drake, brought his *Golden Hind* through Magellan's Straits, then north along

America's west coast, happily raiding Spanish settlements as he went. Had he not previously gathered details
of the Manila galleon route, Drake must surely have
picked up some such information from prisoners collected during his raids. He had learned some Spanish
during his Spanish imprisonment of 1568. Somewhere
near Acapulco, according to chaplain Francis Fletcher,
chronicler of the voyage, "we met with one ship more
(the last we met with in all those coastes) loaded with
linnen, China silke and China dishes, amongst which
wee found also a Faulcon of gold, handsomely wrought,
with a great emerald set in the brest of it."[10]

Possibly inspired by Drake, Thomas Cavendish
(Candish) recorded his own *Famous Voyage . . . Made
Round the Globe of the Earth . . . Begun in the Yeere 1586*
(and ended in 1588). In 1587, having arrived off the
"Cape of California," they lay off and on "until the
fourth of November, on which day in the morning wee
espied the goodly shippe coming from the Philippinas
called Saint Anna the great, being of seven hundred
tunnes: we chased her until noone, so fetching her up,
we gave them fight to the losse of twelve or fourteen of
their men and the spoyle and hurt of many more of
them, whereupon at last they yeelded unto us: In this
conflict we lost only two of our men. So on the sixt of
the sayde November we went into the Port of Agua
Segura, where we ankered and put nine score prisoners
on land: and ransacking the great shippe, we laded our
own two shippes with fourtie tunnes of the chiefest
merchandise, and burnt all the rest, as well the shippe
as goods, to the quantitie of five hundred tunnes of rich
marchandise, because we were not able to bring it away:
This was one of the richest vessels that ever sayled the
Seas, and was able to have made hundreds wealthie, if
we had had meanes to bring it home."[11]

That marchandise could equally well have made
Spaniards wealthy but the Spanish king was too preoc-

cupied with other affairs to worry too much about the loss. Philip II of Spain saw a chance to swallow Portugal, spice empire and all. In the very year that Drake was licking his lips over the seizure of the Manila galleon, the weak and bigoted young Portuguese king, Sebastian I, died and was soon followed to the grave by his royal uncle and legal successor. Into the royal vacuum, Philip promptly projected himself, claiming the Portuguese throne on the grounds that his mother had been a Portuguese princess, as also had been his own first queen. He made himself Philip I of Portugal.

Philip died in 1598, but for about forty years there-after the two crowns remained joined—until, in fact, the Portuguese actively rebelled against their subservience to a Spanish monarch. During the decades of subservi-ence, Portugal's proud empire in the East as well as the spice trade for which so many lives had been sacrificed, was reduced by more than half. The time was clearly at hand for the ascendancy of other imperial-minded Euro-pean lands, including Catholic France and—what would have been a special horror for Philip—heretic England and the Netherlands.

Mariners of these lands had hoped to zero in on Manila itself, but in this, very briefly, the English alone would meet with any success. In 1740, with such a project in mind, Lord Anson was sent out from England with a fleet of six ships. En route, five of them were lost. Nevertheless, Anson in his flagship *Centurion* lingered briefly at Manila before prudence won out. He reim-bursed himself generously with the seizure of the hom-ing galleon *Covadonga* off Cape Espirito Santo on Samar.

It was another British fleet that, in 1762, captured, looted, and occupied Manila only to have to relinquish it a year and a half later when the Seven Years War was ended by a treaty that stipulated the Philippines be returned to Spain. Meanwhile, the Manila galleons had had to add to the many already known risks new dangers

which, without special distinction, the Manileños ascribed to "pirates" of both England and Holland, Lord
Anson being included in that list. Yet, spurred on by
magnificent profits, undeterred by monumental losses,
the stately galleons continued their annual sailing until
1815 when the Napoleonic wars in Europe and wars of
independence in the Americas brought an end to the old
routines.

10

French Challengers

Though the Portuguese had always claimed that the Orient and the sea routes there belonged exclusively to them by a sort of divine right, supported by the sponsorship of a Vicar of Christ, they made no effort to protect that right by keeping secret the expansion of their overseas empire. The boastful displays and noisy public thanksgivings with which they welcomed home the survivors of their maritime enterprises were bound to attract the attention of resident emissaries from neighboring lands. And whether or not those emissaries had reached Lisbon as secret agents, they did not fail to send such exciting news back home to friends and sponsors, who must certainly have resented being outdone by Iberian neighbors.

There had been prior secret attempts on the part of other nationals to push trade, if not conquest, into far lands. Yet the remarkable thing is that for over a century after Vasco da Gama's first voyage, neither Portugal nor Spain had been openly challenged by mariners of other Atlantic-facing lands, notably those of France and England, as well as the Netherlands, which boasted considerable maritime skills.

There may have been many challengers. It is even said that by 1365, fifty years before Prince Henry the Navigator had been able to persuade his Portuguese captains to undertake exploration of the Guinea coast, Dieppe ships had already been there. They brought back, among other items, the Malaguetta pepper which, though not technically identical with the oriental pepper, seemed to appeal to European palates almost as much. French captains also brought home items like the ivory which could so profitably be fashioned into articles for the luxury trade. What the French appear to have left behind on those coasts was a reputation for fair and honorable dealings that was in sharp contrast with the name for ruthlessness the Portuguese earned for themselves.

Dieppe was the Norman French town from which, in 1066, William the Conqueror set forth to appropriate England. The original Norman settlers of that peninsula which faces England's southern coast were Norsemen— adventurous Vikings who found the peninsula a fine base from which to set forth on voyages farther into the Atlantic. But Dieppe was not the only French port from which experienced mariners set forth. Normandy boasted several fine ports, among them Harfleur and Honfleur at the mouth of the Seine. Close to Normandy was the Breton port of St. Malo with Brest, Ushant, and Quimper beyond. With the backcountry devastated by the black death and by wars, Normandy and Brittany were fortunate to be able to look to the sea for sustenance and profit. Voyages of an unrecorded number to various destinations brought back untold wealth. For long, such voyages remained a private venture, French royalty being either myopic to the possibilities of sea power or just reluctant to involve their fortunes in such risky ventures. Local merchant-princes, however, were eager and ready to become involved, motivated not by the impulse to enlarge national empire but by their visions of enlarging profits.

Eventually the French king, Charles VI (1368–1422) made explicit acknowledgment of such Norman achievements, issuing letters patent with the statement, "From our good city of Dieppe, there have always set forth the most experienced of captains and pilots, as well as the ablest and hardiest navigators of Europe and from this place have been made the first discoveries of distant countries."[1] The French king did not indicate exactly what those "distant countries" may have been, perhaps because he was less concerned with creating an overseas empire than in stimulating a desperately needed expansion of trade. In this, secrecy could pay greater dividends than the overpublicizing of achievements.

Perhaps, too, the prudent monarch did not wish to suggest any outright challenge to France's feisty Iberian neighbors, notably Portugal where Prince Henry was already pushing his mariners to explore distant shores. In any case, Charles must have felt caution to be the wisest course with the pestilential black death hardly behind him and the Hundred Years War still raging. France, being looked on with covetous eyes across her long borders to the north and east, could do without adding an outright enemy toward the south and west. There were indeed plenty of good reasons for Charles not to contest empire in the distant Orient.

One of those "ablest and hardiest" navigators mentioned by Charles may have been Binot Palmier de Gonneville who, with a couple of Norman seafaring companions, happened to be in Spain when Vasco da Gama's spice-laden fleet made its triumphant return from his first penetration of the Far East. Here, the three Normans at once perceived, was something very profitable that French mariners had been missing, something they would do well to muscle in on. Losing no time,

Gonneville approached two of Gama's pilots and persuaded them to serve in a venture which, at the moment, existed only in his mind. He knew he would have little difficulty in persuading several prominent citizens of Honfleur to invest in a voyage designed to enrich its sponsors.

On 24 June 1503, Gonneville set sail in the 120-tun *L'Espoir*, heading for the Cape of Good Hope. Off the Guinea coast, they ran into alternating flat calms and wild storms, one of which blew the ship across to the Brazilian coast—purely an accident, the Frenchmen insisted. Arriving there, probably in the region of the river São Francisco do Sul, they settled in for six months or so, making friends with the natives and investigating the land for marketable products. From there, they coasted north to a place since identified as today's Bahia where they remained some months more, again enjoying themselves on shore. Finally, having taken on a cargo of logwood that should find ready sale as a source of much needed dyes to the skilled weavers of their homeland, they sailed for home. This return voyage proved a total disaster, climaxed off the Channel Islands where pirates captured and scuttled the ship. Only twenty-eight of *L'Espoir*'s French crew, including Captain Gonneville, survived to reach home to tell the tale and, perhaps, to point out the "dyewood" potential of Brazil.

If no logwood reached Dieppe from that particular voyage, word of what happened to the cargo certainly did, infuriating native-born shipowner Jean Ango (1480–1551). Ango, of great wealth and Florentine lifestyle, was as fascinating and picturesque as were the decades through which he lived. He was a mere eight years old when, in 1488, Bartholomew Dias brought his caravels back to Portugal from his epochal discovery that there was a negotiable sea route around the southernmost tip of Africa. Ango was a teenager of thirteen when Columbus returned to Spain from his equally epochal voyage of discovery. Even though news could travel no faster than horse-drawn post coaches or wind-powered coasting vessels, news of these ventures must soon have reached the Norman coast and set aflame the minds of adventurous citizens, young and old. By the time he reached manhood, Jean Ango was becoming one of the most influential shipowners on that coast, prepared to sponsor great ventures that would outrival the Portuguese and Spanish. Like the Portuguese Prince Henry of the previous century, this prince-merchant set up his own court facing the sea and there gathered poets, mariners, ship masters, mapmakers, and shipmasters turned corsairs. The talk there ran to past adventures, newly acquired knowledge, and future plans. So influential was Ango that he was popularly acclaimed, "Vicomte de Dieppe."

Ango's ships played their part in all the maritime wars which France was conducting with her neighbors. Finally, in 1544 and 1545, Ango took personal charge of the naval operations against England, ruining himself with the enormous personal advances he made against the expenses of the war which the royal treasury neglected to repay. He died in 1551, still disputing the debts, in his chateau in Dieppe. His son, a second Jean Ango, carried on as best he could the maritime tradition established by his father.

Two of the mariners encouraged by the Angos were to have great influence on the future of North America. Typically, they were reaching out to grasp the commodities of the Far East by finding an easily navigable strait they believed must exist across the continent that so inconsiderately blocked the way to "blessed Cathay" of silken and spicy charms.

The first of those two mariners was, like so many early navigators, of Italian extraction—Giovanni Verrazzano. Born to a mercantile Venetian family residing in Lyons, the silk emporium of France as it was to remain for centuries, Verrazzano's eyes soon focused on China and her legendary silks. He was well educated and had become familiar with both mercantile and marine skills by the year 1520 when he won sponsorship by the silk merchants of the Lyons Italian enclave. He also acquired a commission from the French king, Francis I, for a voyage that was to improve upon Magellan's recent exploit by finding a shorter, more northerly route to China.

On his return from that voyage, begun in 1524, Verrazzano reported to the French king that his intention on this voyage was to reach Cathay and the east coast of Asia and that he did not expect to find such an obstacle of new land as he found. The extent of that land and of the great ocean separating it from Asia were still beyond most men's imaginings. Without finding any silks, spices, or golden wealth to encourage his efforts, Verrazzano coasted north from just above the peninsula that now bears the name Florida to the Cape Breton peninsula, then gave up for the time being and sailed for home.

In June 1525, Verrazzano, still hopeful, again sailed westward, taking three ships destined, he believed, for the Indies with spices, as well as silks, now on the agenda. This voyage involved sailing toward the mouth of the Amazon, then coasting south to Magellan's Straits which Verrazzano failed to negotiate. Frustrated, he decided to risk Portuguese antagonism by taking the Cape of Good Hope route but beyond the cape the fleet became scattered in a storm. Finally Verrazzano crossed back to Brazil where he loaded a cargo of dyewood and headed for home.

Still convinced he was destined to find the elusive northern passage to China and now encouraged by the fact that, failing to locate it, he could at least sweeten failure by delivering to his sponsors a remunerative cargo of dyewood, Giovanni Verrazzano and his mapmaking brother Gerolamo again set forth in 1527. Reaching a

Caribbean island, probably Santo Domingo, and misled by the friendly reception he had previously experienced along the North American coast, Giovanni waded ashore from the ship's boat to waiting natives who promptly attacked him, killed him and ate his remains before the horrified eyes of his helplessly watching brother and shipmates. Thus ended this gifted mariner who, in spite of his failure to reach Cathay, left behind the then almost unique achievement of describing the appearance and manners of natives he encountered along the North American shore. It would remain for later, more fortunate French explorers to penetrate those shores more deeply.

The Angos were not to be dissuaded by the failure of a single mariner. That more northerly passage to China simply must exist and one of their own navigators would surely locate it. The next known navigator to become involved in this undertaking received prompt royal sponsorship. In 1532, when King Francis I (1494–1547) was making a pilgrimage to the famous abbey of Mont St. Michel, he was introduced to a relative of the abbey's treasurer. This man—Jacques Cartier (149?–1552)—the king was told, had made voyages to the Newfoundland fishing grounds and to Brazil and might be just the man to bring off discovery of the new strait leading to China.

The pious king was impressed. There remained an obstacle which even the magnificent abbot of Mont St. Michel had to acknowledge—the nearly forty-year-old bull of Pope Alexander VI dividing all the overseas world between Portugal and Spain. There was, however, no obstacle to having that bull reinterpreted. In 1532, the reigning pope, Clement VII, was a Medici by birth and a French ally by political as well as matrimonial ties—the pope's niece was about to marry the French king's son. It was not too difficult to persuade him to announce that the Alexandrine bull was meant to apply only to lands already discovered in 1494 when the original treaty was drawn up. Thus, neatly North America—Canada specifically—became available for French acquisition. (Incidentally, this new interpretation would remove the still-to-be-discovered Falkland Islands, first sighted in 1592 by the Englishman John Davis, from the jurisdiction of Spain and her heirs).

In any case, a way was thus opened for the French king to commission Jacques Cartier's proposed voyage of discovery. In April 1534, Cartier set sail from St. Malo, surely with the blessing and possibly some support from the Angos. In the course of three voyages, he explored eastern Canada including the St. Lawrence River. China, however, remained inaccessibly beyond the rapids above today's Montreal, which ships could not pass. These rapids, being the nearest approach to China Cartier managed, have been ironically baptized "Lachine." Cartier's real achievement, viewed from this distance in time, was to open northern North America for French colonization.

Pope Clements reinterpretation of the Alexandrine bull must have been music to the ears of the Angos and their mariners. It legitimatized the exploration that had been going on for years, since none of them had accepted the notion that the whole world beyond the seas must officially belong to Spain and Portugal. In view of Portugal's claim to exclusive use of all known sea routes to the East, Norman vessels had had to be equipped to fight off possible attacks with defensive weaponry which could easily be turned to offensive use, especially when heavily laden prizes could be intercepted on homeward voyages. Pilots and pirates were often indistinguishable from each other.

One of Jean Ango's famed pilots was Jean Parmentier, a gifted poet-navigator about whose life, as with most Ango mariners, there is considerable mystery. In 1525, two Parmentier brothers started on a voyage that took them to Florida, the West Indies, Brazil and Madagascar. One thousand leagues beyond that island, they reached Sumatra where, right under Portuguese noses, they bargained for spices.

Observing the Portuguese with unfriendly eyes, Jean Parmentier recorded, "If the Portuguese, who claim to be masters of these lands, had had in mind the glory of religion, rather than the love of gain, one half at least of these people would have embraced Christianity, for many are anxious to understand our religion." Again, and rather imprecisely, of Portugal: "Although this nation is the smallest on the globe, the whole world is not large enough to satisfy their cupidity."[2] Having thus filled their minds with impressions and their ships' holds "with pepper and other spices, we left for Dieppe, where we arrived safely after a long and dangerous navigation."

Soon after the Parmentiers reached home in 1527, they decided to try for bigger stakes still farther to the east, China and her silks being the ultimate goal. Their voyage ended in disaster with the deaths of both Parmentiers. However, it did little to dampen the nautical ardor of the Normans who had long recognized the sea to be a fickle mistress. Ango's vessels continued to frequent the Brazilian coast for cargoes of dyewood, though just how many vessels and voyages were involved remained one of those trade secrets which the Angos were so skilled in guarding.

For Portugal, this was doubly hurtful, wounding both the national exchequer and the national pride. By the time of the Parmentiers' 1527 voyage, King John of Portugal was finding French insolence so intolerable that he issued peremptory orders that all French ships be swept from the seas. What became of the French ships then on their way to Brazil? It presently leaked out that the Portuguese had seized three French ships loading dyewood in Bahia, taking captive about 300 French mariners. Some of these captives were hung, others buried in sand to their shoulders, then used for target practice by Portuguese arquebusiers. A few were handed over to the natives to supply them with a French feast.

Such an act of vicarious cannibalism could hardly be ignored even by the reluctantly hostile French monarch. At long last, Francis took official notice of the situation and made it a national matter by issuing Letters of Marque and Reprisal—such letters being defined as "an incomplete state of war." Incomplete or not, they supplied legitimacy for retaliatory French attacks on Portuguese vessels homeward bound with rich Far Eastern cargoes. Thus, by a semi-piratical route, spice cargoes reached French ports, making Frenchmen increasingly aware of the riches other nationals were reaping by virtue of their maritime prowess. Inevitably, the French grew increasingly determined to have for themselves a piece of the spice pie, though for another three-quarters of a century nothing was done nationally to that end.

Pyrard de Laval, a Frenchman who shipped for India in 1601 aboard a French vessel that was destined to pile up on the Maldive Islands, spoke for many compatriots when he summed up the state of affairs in the opening paragraphs of his journal of the voyage and its aftermath.

> The abundance of all kinds of wealth which France produces, and the favors which the bounty of Heaven hath so liberally poured upon her soil, may have been the cause why the French have so long neglected the sea. They have enough to do with the land . . . and take no thought to seek more amid the perils of a treacherous sea. . . . Yet, in truth, France, in neglecting trade, deprives herself of riches . . . for she is washed by two productive seas and furnished with many good harbors, by means of which she might communicate and negotiate

with many nations far from her coasts, as
though they were her neighbors, on the east
and on the west, and even with the most distant
countries. . . . We are now seeing our mistake,
for the French, after neglecting countless fair
opportunities (which the Portuguese and Spaniards have not only taken but sought) are con-
strained to receive from those nations, in retail,
gold, spices, and curious things of the East, in
place of having fetched themselves and distrib-
uting them to others. So at present the Portuguese and Spaniards are trying to keep to
themselves those elements which are common
to all, and by all manner of wrongdoing to
chase from the seas the French and other
nations who would voyage and traffic therein.[3]

On 16 May 1601, Pyrard left the port at St. Malo in
a ship whose sponsors were hoping to test the profitabil-
ity of the role of middlemen of trade in "those curious
things of the East." It was to be an unsuccessful voyage
from the start: "When we were but nine or ten leagues
to sea the foremast of our ship split and broke in half,
and this was the beginning of our misfortune. . . . As for
me, I never had a good opinion of our voyage on account
of . . . the bad order and discipline in the ships; for there
was no piety or devotion, but plenty of oaths and blasphemy, disobedience to the officers, mutiny and care-
lessness, and every day quarrelling, assaults, thefts, and
the like vices. . . . The Flemings and Hollanders never
let offences go unpunished on board their ships, which
is the cause their voyages succeed better." Another
contributing cause to the greater maritime successes of
those Hollanders was that they seemed to have discovered how to complete a voyage without losing their crews
to scurvy—"a great number on board our vessels but
among the Hollanders not a man."[4]

By 24 August Pyrard was experiencing the heat and bad weather of equatorial seas: "The heat is violent and stifling in the extreme; it destroys most of the provisions; the water becomes putrid and full of big worms; all kinds of meat and fish go bad, even the most carefully salted; all the butter we had melted to oil, and so were the tallow candles; the ships began to split in those parts which were not under water; the pitch and tar likewise melted; and it was impossible to remain below as in an oven."[5] All this was aggravated by weather which was "inconstancy itself" as flat calms alternated with violent storms.

It was in one such storm that the ship piled up on the Maldive Islands, a group to the southwest of the southern tip of India over which the Portuguese claimed sovereignty. Pyrard and a few other French survivors were picked up and taken to Goa anticipating imprisonment, at best, with no hope of ever seeing France again. However, shrewdly assessing the qualities of his captors, Pyrard won his way to freedom and, finally, permission to return home, by taking service in the Portuguese army in India.

All the time, while feigning stupidity, the Frenchman mentally recorded a host of fascinating details of contemporary life in remote Portuguese outposts like Goa. Had it occurred to the ever suspicious Portuguese officials that the dumb Frenchman would publish an account of his eight years' residence in Portuguese India, they would not have permitted him to survive, much less to return home.

Despite survival problems, Pyrard lost no chance to assess the commercial possibilities in the Portuguese Far Eastern empire: "Pepper grows in abundance at Cochin, Cannanor, Barcelor, and all along the Malabar Coast. It is thence the Portuguese take it, and none others dare buy it in those parts. There is also a great store of it in the islands of Sumatra and Java, whence the Arabs and all other Indians, and latterly the Hollanders, English, and others that voyage thither, in despite of the King of Spain, supply themselves withal; it is bigger and heavier than that of Malabar, and the Indians prize it more; the Portuguese, however, boast theirs to be the best."[6]

Ginger was "commoner than pepper. . . . The King of Spain prohibits the export of it in bulk, because it would interfere with the sale of his pepper, inasmuch as many would content themselves with the former."[7] Nutmegs, mace, cinnamon, and cloves are also discussed, though neither Spain nor Portugal—both then under the same king—are specifically mentioned as monopolizing them. The general meaning, however, is clear. Other greedy monarchs had been doing the French out of a possibly highly profitable trade. There could have been many reasons why the French monarch failed to react effectively to Pyrard's account once it was brought to his attention. One possibility was the attitude so haughtily expressed during the following century by Louis XV: "We make was as a king, not as a merchant," while his spendthrift lifestyle hastened the day when a French king must turn to merchants for aid.

Whatever the lack of royal response to Pyrard's account, French merchants were quick to get the message which, of course, some of them had already been acting upon, as also had the Dutch and the English. By the first years of the seventeenth century, the English and Dutch had organized trading companies that were to become powerful political as well as financial institutions. The French would organize their own company only in 1663 and even then their Far Eastern factories, such as Pondicherry, did not constitute serious competition to other European lands. Yet eventually it was to be an innovative Frenchman, appropriately named Peter Pepper (Pierre Poivre, 1719–1776) who launched a scheme, involving none of the violent military confrontations spice rivalry had so often engendered, that would bring an end to all those Far Eastern spice monopolies and to the spice empires they had bred. At the heart of this scheme lay recognition of the simple fact that plants could be transplanted!

But all that was to come much later, over a century after those "Hollanders" and English had extended their activities and rivalries to the Far East.

11

The Shortest Way

It was the talk of the town in 1522 when, after a three years' absence, Elcano brought the *Victoria* up the Guadalquivir to drop anchor near Seville. The fact that she was the worn-out survivor of a fleet of five vessels, that her captain, Magellan, had been slaughtered on a remote island he had discovered, and that hundreds of other lives had been lost along the way, seemed to count as nothing against the fortune in spices that the *Victoria* brought in her hold. Even Seville's poorest citizen could appreciate that.

What it took more discriminating minds to appreciate was the fact that she had sailed west to find a passage through the land mass barring her way, that she had actually reached the spice-rich East, and had finally made it back to Spain, still sailing in a westerly direction. Of course the talk was not confined to Spain. The news spread fast with the English response being, as Sebastian Cabot suggested, "all men with great admiration affirmed it to bee a thing more divine than humane, to

saile by the West into the East where spices growe, by a
way that was never knowen before."[1]

Surely, the growing number of increasingly adventurous mariners came to believe, all ways could not yet
be known. Portugal claimed as uniquely hers the eastward route that took ships around the Cape of Good
Hope, while Spain had just grabbed the westerly route.
But the delightful thing about this newly accepted belief
that the earth was a sphere was that if you started from
any point on a globe and kept heading in a single
direction—followed a "great circle," that is—you would
eventually arrive back at your starting point. The direction need not be east or west but could equally be south
or north or any compass direction in between. The
north, in fact, seemed to offer the shortest route of all,
as navigators were soon to persuade themselves. They
had reason on their side—that is, as long as they just
studied their globes—but they had no practical knowledge of conditions that might be encountered along
northern routes and would have to learn the hard way.

Merchants were at least as excited as mariners by
the newly envisaged possibilities of a quick and easy
passage to the East. Especially excited were the foreign
merchants who resided in Seville, that busy commercial
city where merchants of less fortunate kingdoms gathered to purchase oriental commodities for redistribution
in their own lands. Made uncomfortably and constantly
aware of their inferior national status, they were bound
to relish all possible means for circumventing the arro-
gant Spanish.

An English merchant residing in Seville became
increasingly convinced that his king was missing a good
thing if not an altogether sure one. Considering the
matter and studying such maps and globes as he could
lay hands on, merchant Robert Thorne decided to record
his thoughts and observations for the benefit of his king.
It would not have been proper for him to address the

king directly, but he could do so through the English "Lord Ambassadour for king Henrie the eight to Charles the Emperour" and this he did at considerable length "in the yeere 1527." He began by pointing out that "of the new trade of the Spicerie of the Emperour, there is no doubt but that the Islands are fertile of cloves, Nutmegs, Mace, Cinnamom: and that the said Islands, with other there about, abound with golde, Rubies, Diamonds."

After dwelling at some length on the great value of the commodities to be gathered in those islands, he lets it be known that he himself had not been idle in pursuing direct dealings with the Spice Islands: "In a flote of three shippes and a caravell that went from this citie armed by the merchants of it, which departed Aprill last past, I and my partener have one thousand foure hundred duckets that we employed in said fleete, principally for that two Englishmen, friends of mine, which are somewhat learned in Cosmographie, should goe in the same shippes, to bring me certaine relation of the situation of the countrey and to be expert in the navigation of those seas. . . . Seeing in these quarters are shippes and mariners of that countrey, and cardes [charts] by which they saile, though much unlike ours: that they should procure to have said cards, and learne how to understand them: and especially to know what navigation they have for those islands."

While his friends were happily spying out navigational details in Far Eastern seas, merchant Thorne's mind was busy with other schemes inspired by his study of such world maps and globes as were available: "Nowe then . . . there is no doubt but sayling Northwards and passing the Pole, descending to the Equinoctiall line, we shall hitte these Islandes, and it should be a much shorter way than either the Spaniards or the Portingalls have. . . . God knoweth that though by it I shoulde have no great interest, yet I have had and still have no little mind of this businesse so that if I had facultie to my will, it shoulde be the first thing that I woulde understande, even to attempt, if our Seas Northwards be Navigable to the Pole or no."[2]

Even in 1527 things could be made to move fast if the purpose was to enlarge a king's wealth and empire. By May of that year, as Richard Hakluyt reported, two ships, "whereof one was called the *Dominus vobiscum*, set out . . . for the discoverie of the North partes." Hakluyt stated further that: "Master Robert Thorne of Bristoll, a notable member and ornament of his countrey . . . in a letter of his to king Henry the 8 . . . exhorted the foresaid king with very waightie and substantiall reasons, to set forth a discoverie even to the North pole. . . . This same moneth (they say) king Henry the 8 sent two faire ships well manned and victualled, having in them diverse cunning men to seeke strange regions, and so they set foorth out of the Thames, the 20 day of May, in the 19 yeere of his raigne which was the yeere of Our Lord 1527."[3]

Hakluyt later attempted in vain to find and talk with men who had been on that voyage. Finally, second- or thirdhand, he learned that "one of the ships was cast away as it entered into a dangerous gulphe . . . whereupon the other ship shaping her course for the coast of Norumbega, oftentimes putting their men on land to search the state of those unknowen regions, returned home about the beginning of October, of the yeere aforesaid. And thus much (by reason of the great negligence of the writers of those times who should have used more care in preserving the memories of the worthie acts of our nation,) is all that hitherto I can learne, or find out of this voiage."[4] Thus, ingloriously, ended the first English attempt to find that elusive passage through the "North partes."

There is now no way of discovering whether or when other such attempts may have been made, but it is safe to guess that had any been made immediately, it would have been talked about and that some of the talk would have reached the alert ears of Richard Hakluyt. Mariners, had they been so occupied, would have let Hakluyt know, but they were not likely to have had in their own pockets the money needed to buy and equip ships and engage crews. No matter how alluring it may have seemed to be first to open a new and shorter passage to Cathay, they would have had to turn to merchants to back such a voyage. The prospect was beginning to look most alluring to the merchants too.

The motive was as old as trade itself: "At what time our Marchants perceived the commodities and wares of England to be in small request with the Countreis and people about us, and neere unto us, and that those Marchandises which strangers in the time and memorie of our ancestors did earnestly seeke and desire, were now neglected, and the price thereof abated, although by us caried to their owne portes, and all forreine marchandises in great accompt, and their prices wonderfully raised: certaine grave citizens of London, and men of great wisedome, and careful of the good of their Countrey, beganne to thinke with themselves, how this mischief might be remedied . . . it was at last concluded that three shippes should be prepared and furnished out, for the search and discoverie of the Northern part of the worlde, to open a way and passage to our men for travaile to new and unknowen kingdomes."[5]

They organized themselves into a company in 1553 to promote a "newe Navigation and discoverie of the Kingdome of Muscovia by the Northeast." They offered membership to any private individual who had twenty-five pounds to invest, and with these funds purchased three ships, outfitted them, engaged crews and officers. In May 1553, amid general excitement and with a display worthy of Spain or Portugal, the three ships sailed gaily off. Two of them were found a year later by fishermen off the coast of Lapland, the men's bodies emaciated and frozen stiff. The third ship, commanded by Richard Chancellor, had been separated from those two in a storm and eventually reached the far northern Russian port of Arkhangelsk, whence Chancellor proceeded by sled to Moscow. Being one of the earliest English travellers to reach the city, he reported on it in some detail. Never forgetting his backers, Chancellor arranged a trade treaty with imperial Russia before returning home to help organize "The Worshipful Company of Merchants Trading in Russia"—more generally known as the Muscovy Company. The second voyage to Russia which Chancellor planned ended in disaster when his ship was wrecked off the Scottish coast and he lost his life.

Russian trade, heavily slanted toward turning English commodities into furs of value, and vice versa, continued for enough years to enable enterprising English merchant-travellers to penetrate as far as the Caspian Sea and cross it into Persia. Anthony Jenkinson, one of the most enterprising of the merchants, recorded a list of countries visited between his first voyage in October 1546 and "the yeere of our Lord, 1572, when I returned last out of Russia." After listing European and Mediterranean lands thus visited, Jenkinson continues, "I have sailed farre Northward within the Mare glaciale, where wee have had continuall day, and sight of the Sunne ten weekes together, and that navigation was in Norway, and Lapland Samagotia, and other very strange places. I have travelled through all the ample dominions of the Emperour of Russia and Moscovia, which extend from the North sea, and the confines of Norway, and Lapland, even to the Mare Caspian. . . . I have sailed over the Caspian sea, and discovered all the regions thereabout Adjacent. . . . I have travelled 40 daies journey beyond the said sea, toward the Orientall India and Cathaia, through divers deserts and wildernesses . . . not without great perils and dangers sundry times."

Finally, "being wearie and growing old, I am content to take my rest in mine owne house, chiefly comforting my selfe, in that my service hath bene honourably accepted and rewarded of her majestie and the rest by whom I have bene emploied."[6]

Jenkinson's list of lands visited would have been notable in any century, especially in light of the difficulties of travel and the real personal risks. Another sixteenth-century visitor to Persia proclaimed that he would far rather be a beggar all his life in England than a wealthy merchant for seven years in Moslem Persia where the feeling toward people of other religions was no less antagonistic than it remains today in Persia's successor nation—Iran.

Particularly fascinating is Jenkinson's list of trade goods—items he could profitably dispose of and those he might secure for home trade. He could, he found, sell woolens, red cloth, copper, and "Brasilis," which may have been dyewood. This looks like a pretty skimpy list to generate the means for purchasing the available oriental commodities as listed by him—raw silk, pepper, ginger, nutmegs, cloves; as well as rice and alum. Especially intriguing is "yew for bowe staves."[7] Had those famous English archers so exhausted the English-grown yew available as to persuade English merchants to secure yew from halfway around the world? However that may be, the overland trade for Eastern commodities was doomed.

Though few of the courageous English mariners who headed into the north were, like Anthony Jenkinson, to survive to retire and "take my rest in mine own home," the dream of a shorter northern passage to the Far East was to die hard even after most Englishmen acknowledged that they were not likely to discover a navigable northeast passage. There still remained, however, the hope for a navigable northwest passage—a hope which would never quite die until centuries had passed and still more brave men had left their wrecked ships and frozen remains in the far north. Name an English mariner of note in the late sixteenth century and you may be almost certain that if he had not spent his life harassing the Spanish off one American coast or the other, he had at least once tried his hand at circumventing the Spanish by seeking for that longed-for polar route or, at least, a northwest passage.

Outstanding among such English navigators was John Davis whose name and fame are less known today than are the names of more publicity-conscious men like Frobisher, Raleigh, and the Gilberts. Yet Davis won from a twentieth-century mariner of note, Admiral Samuel Eliot Morison, the most unstinting praise as, "no more just, courageous, and wise seaman than Davis ever sailed under the Cross of St. George."[8] In the years 1585 to 1587, Davis made three northern voyages, finding no northwest passage but so large a haul of fish that Englishmen soon came to appreciate the value of the Newfoundland fisheries—highly profitable, if not quite the gold, jewels, and spices hoped for. Davis never gave up his belief in the existence of a navigable passage to the north of America but after three unsuccessful voyages, the merchant-adventurers back home who had been supplying funds decided they had had enough. This skilled navigator had then to find other backing. He, as other Englishmen were presently to do, found it in the Netherlands, though this Dutch voyage was not to be toward the north.

The Dutch who, for reasons of religion, were closer to the English than were most European nations, were aware of their need for skilled and experienced navigators. They were glad to engage the services of experienced English mariners who might be temporarily out of employment. The Dutch need of mariners is apparent in a petition for the remission of taxes submitted by the States of Holland to the Emperor Charles V, who reigned from 1519 to 1556. The petition stated that Holland is very small, both in length and breadth, almost with three sides exposed to the sea, and full of downs, swamps, turf-moors, lakes and other unfruitful places, where one can neither sow grain nor raise cattle; wherefore the inhabitants, to find food for their wives and children, were obliged to go and trade and traffic in foreign ports, and to export certain tissues—i.e. textiles—for which reasons the principal profession of the country had to be the art of navigation and the sea trade.

For the Dutch, even more than for the English, it was vital to keep open international channels of trade. When, in the 1590s, Charles's son Philip decided to deny Dutch ships access to Spanish and Portuguese ports, they had no alternative, if they wished to survive, but to seek other ways of securing the commodities they had been obtaining there. The presumed northern route to Cathay, which the English had been eyeing for decades, immediately came to the fore in the minds of progressive Dutchmen. They were further stimulated by Jan Huyghen van Linschoten's account of the Portuguese East which, though not officially published until 1596, was generally known a few years earlier. They believed that if they could reach the East, they might possibly carve out there an empire for themselves. If that should mean carving bits and pieces out of the Portuguese and Spanish holdings, then the Dutch could find no cause for sorrow in that.

Like the English, the Dutch saw the southern routes closed to them unless they were prepared to challenge the biggest and most powerful navies of their time. Also like the English, they saw the northern route as leading directly from their own harbors to Cathay and the Spice Islands. The first known Dutch Arctic voyagers sailed in 1584 and, although they got no nearer Cathay than northeast Russia, they managed to load a valuable cargo of furs, rock crystal, and glass. They lost it, however, when their ship was wrecked in the shallow mouth of the Pechora River. The navigator of that lost ship—Brussels-born Netherlands citizen Oliver Brunel— then offered his services to the king of Denmark in trying to locate the lost Greenland colonies. After three vain attempts, the search was given up, whereupon Brunel, in the footloose pattern of sixteenth-century navigators, is said to have offered his services to the English.

It was not until the 1590s that a sizable expedition was fitted out in Holland for the purpose of seeking the passage to the northeast. The attempt was repeated annually for three years—1594, 1595, 1596. The 1594 fleet included four ships—two from Amsterdam, one from Zeeland, one from Enkhuizen, "whereof William Barents, a notable skilfull and wise pilote, was commander over the ships of Amsterdam."[9] As supercargo and journal keeper, went Jan Huyghen van Linschoten, whose book had helped inspire the voyage. They set sail in the last days of May 1594, headed northeast, and arrived near Novaya Zemlya off the Siberian coast when, "thinking that they had discovered enough for that time, and that it was too late in the yeare to saile any further, as also that their commission was to discover the scituation, and to come home againe before winter . . . they turned again"[10] and headed for hom, arriving in mid-September.

Linschoten was again supercargo on one of the seven ships sent out the next year. In both the 1595 and 1596 fleets—the latter of two vessels only—Barents was commander. Sailing in June 1595, the second fleet was back home in early November, again without profit or success insofar as the desired passage was concerned.

By the next spring, the States General of the Netherlands had decided not to help finance further voyages to the northeast but announced that if anyone or group wished to underwrite a voyage at their own expense and should succeed therein, generous reward might be expected from the States General. Still cherishing a belief in that route, William Barents again served with two Amsterdam vessels under him.

They set sail in mid-May and soon learned some interesting facts of natural history, quite new to them. They encountered polar bears so huge and ferocious that two men were killed, one by his head being bitten off, before the Dutchmen learned to keep their distance. Most revealing of the limited biological knowledge of those days are the comments on the Brent geese whose nesting habits the mariners could observe at firsthand in the far north. "Those geese," wrote the journal keeper, Gerrit de Veer, "were such as come into Holland about Weiringen, and every yeare are there taken in abundance, but till this time it was never knowne where they laid and hatcht their egges; so that some men have taken upon them to write that they grow upon trees in Scotland, that hang over the water, and those branches which hang over the water, and the fruit of which falls into the water, become young geese and swim away, but those that fall upon land burst in sunder and come to nothing: but this is now found to be false, and it is not to bee wondered at that no man could tell where they lay their egges, for that no man that ever we knew had ever been under 80 degrees, nor that land under 80 degrees was never set down in any chart, much lesse the geese that breed therein."[11]

A storm separated the two ships and Barents's went on alone, to be frozen in the ice off Novaya Zemlya, near the Siberian coast, by early September. On 11 September, Gerrit de Veer recorded: "at last we sawe that we could not get out of the ice but rather became faster, and could not loose our ship as at other times we had done, as also that it began to be winter, we took counsell together what we were best to doe according to the circumstances of the time, in order that we might winter there and attend such adventure as God would send us: and after we had debated upon the matter, to keepe and defend ourselves both from the cold and the wild beastes, we determined to build a house upon the land, to keep us therein as well as we could."[12]

They located driftwood which "served us not onely to build our house, but also to burn and serve us all the winter long; otherwise without all doubt we had died there miserably with extreme cold." At this juncture, their carpenter died, but the others—sixteen strong when all were able to work—hauled the driftwood for framing their house and then, in early October, removed planks from the ship for roofing and siding. The house was completed barely in time for a great snowstorm that began on 8 October. From the first week of November until the last week of January, they had the new experience of not seeing the sun at all. None died during the winter though malnutrition and scurvy took their toll of strength.

They kept their spirits up by planning how to get their ship free from the ice in the spring, but by June they despaired of this and made plans to leave her and set out for home in the ship's boat and "scute" (scow?). They composed a letter to be left behind in their hut, in case some other men should some time pass that way. It was to be 275 years before Norwegian captain Elling Carlsen would find the Dutchmen's house on Novaya Zemlya, gather the articles left behind, insofar as they remained in a state to be moved, and thus establish beyond question the actual place where Barents and his party had passed the winter of 1596–1597.

Gerrit de Veer kept a copy of that note and included it in his report. It runs, in part, as follows:

Having till this day stayd for the time and opportunity, in hope to get our ship loose, whereof there is now little or no hope. . . . And

for that it seemed almost impossible to get the
ship out of the ice, therefore I and William
Barents, and the other officers and company of
sailors thereunto belonging, considering with
ourselves which could be the best course for us
to save our owne lives and some wares belonging to the merchants, we could find no better
meanes than to mend our boat and scute, and
to provide our selves as well as could of all
things necessarie, that being ready we might
not loose or overslip any fit time and opportunity that God should send us; for that it was
requisite for us to take the fittest time, otherwise we should surely have perished with hunger and cold, which as yet is to be feared will
goe hard inough with us, for that there are
three or foure of us from whom in our work we
have no help, and the best and strongest of us
are so weake with the great cold and diseases
that we have so long time endured, that we
have but halfe a man's strength; and it is to be
feared that it will rather be worse than better,
in regard of the long voiage that we have in
hand, and our bread will not last us longer than
to the moneth of August.[13]

Realizing that only with a prompt departure could
they hope to reach people who could add to their scanty
supplies, and finding the ship "as fast as ever inclosed in
the ice," they composed their letter on 1 June 1597. By
13 June, all had signed it—all of the fifteen left, that is,
who were literate (four names were lacking). William
Barents's signature is there, though he was already at
death's door and was to die within a week after the group
set out. Another man died the same day and yet another
a week later. All the others survived, with the help of
supplies shared with them by Russian seal and whale

hunters they met. Finally, they encountered a Dutch ship—skippered, to their surprise, by the man they had thought lost in the storm the previous year—and were taken home to Amsterdam, where they arrived 1 November 1597.

As touching as it is to read words composed in icy wastes, which many of the signers must have feared were never destined for any eyes but their own, it is even more touching that they should have set out on that grim journey, which they knew was to demand the utmost in courage and endurance, with the thought not only of saving "our own lives" but also "some of the wares belonging to the merchants" to whom they felt under obligation. All Dutch were painfully aware that the survival of their native land itself, fully as much as their own personal survival, depended upon their merchants. Whatever might happen to their northern ventures, the Dutch, both merchants and mariners, kept their eyes focused on Cathay and the Spice Islands of the East.

As the northeast passage, like the polar one, came to seem all but hopeless to the sixteenth-century navigators of both England and the Netherlands, they all zeroed in seriously on the northwest. The resulting awareness of North America, even though those voyages added little to the silks and spices available on European markets, actually would have more enduring and far-reaching consequences than access to either kind of perishable commodity. Verrazzano and Cartier showed the way for France, scouting the shores of the new continent and pointing out the possibilities for settlements which might more than pay for themselves with furs. One navigator after another had sought a northwest passage before Dutch and English colonists began making themselves at home farther to the south on the same continent that had blocked their passage to the South Sea.

Inevitably, both the Dutch and English were to

challenge, on the high seas, the Spanish-Portuguese monopoly of the southern routes. Yet the hope and the search for that northern passage continued—a search epitomized in the life and death of one man more than any other. This was the Englishman Henry Hudson who, in the course of four northern voyages, served both England and Holland and tried all the proposed routes. Hudson's first voyage, undertaken for English sponsors, was an over-the-Pole attempt in 1607. The second voyage, of 1608, also under English sponsorship, was toward the northeast, as also was the third under Dutch sponsorship. Finally acknowledging defeat in that direction, Hudson sailed in 1610 in command of English ships for a try at a northwestern passage. On this voyage, he located three bodies of water that still bear his name— Hudson River, Hudson's Straits, Hudson's Bay. In the bay, his crew mutinied and set him, his son John, and seven other men adrift in the ship's boat, never to be heard from again.

Since those times, many attempts have been made to locate a practical navigable northern passage, though in the last century the motive has been adventure rather than trade in Eastern commodities. In 1879, the Norwegian Captain Nordenskjöld took the *Vega* by a northeast passage through to the Bering Sea. In the first years of this century, the Norwegian captain Roald Amundsen took the *Gjøa* through a northwest route on a voyage of several years duration, his ship being frozen in the ice during three winters. Along the way, the *Gjøa*'s commander encountered the skeletal remains of earlier adventurers.

The polar route, never achieved by sailing ships, now serves as a route for airplanes that can fly above the forbidding expanses of ice and snow. But those silks and spices which inspired it all still come to us, if they come from the East at all, by longer, milder southerly routes.

12

The Unchained Lion

In 1517, while Magellan was dickering with the Spanish king for backing of his proposed voyage through a yet-to-be-discovered strait, an Augustinian monk in Germany was venturing into equally uncertain and dangerous waters without leaving his homeland. That monk, Martin Luther, shocked the contemporary world with his ninety-five articles against ecclesiastical corruption which he nailed to the door of the court church in Wittenberg.

Four years later, while the devout Magellan was striving to convert to Christianity the pagan dwellers in a newly discovered Far Eastern archipelago, a no less devout Martin Luther was summoned to face the imperial Diet of Worms. There he was called upon to defend himself, if possible, against an all-powerful ecclesiastical hierarchy presided over by Charles, king of Spain, in his role as Holy Roman Emperor. Both Magellan and Luther believed themselves to be devout and loyal Catholics and if the events just mentioned seem to have had no other possible connection, their joint consequences were to have great and unanticipated repercussions not only in Europe but also in those far lands toward which Magellan was undertaking to navigate.

That Luther survived the ordeal he was subjected to at Worms was not due to the leniency of his ecclesiastical judges but to the protection of the princely Elector of Saxony who belonged to that gradually increasing number of brave people who had dared risk accusations of heresy by appearing to side with Luther. Reformation of the Roman Catholic Church, which had been quietly simmering in men's minds for some years, was given new form and urgency by Luther's courageous defense of his theses. Dissident Catholics of many lands took part, even though they knew the price of dissent to be relentless persecution. Particularly receptive to reform in the Catholic church were the Netherlanders, who had lived for so long under the rule of a Spanish monarch who, as hereditary Duke of Burgundy, considered the Netherlands as his personal property. When it came to his notice that his Dutch subjects were embracing the new Protestantism, Charles was bound to eliminate these heretics in any way possible.

Charles's edict, issued after the meeting at Worms, forecast things to come: "As it appears that the aforesaid Martin is not a man but a devil under the form of a man, and clothed in the dress of a priest, the better to bring the human race to hell and damnation, therefore all his disciples are to be punished with death and forfeiture of all their goods."[1] This did not imply judicial condemnation, to be followed by hanging, but the seizure of persons under suspicion, torture to extract confessions, burning alive, and the use of any other methods the ingenious inquisitorial mind could invent. The holocaust over which Charles and his minions proudly presided had the predictable consequence of fixing the heretics' minds on their heresy.

Motley, historian of the Netherlands, summed it up

succinctly: "The fires were kept constantly supplied with human fuel by monks who knew the art of burning reformers better than that of arguing with them. . . . Still, the people remained unconvinced. Thousands of burned heretics had not made a single convert"[2] to the emperor's orthodoxy. In fact, that constantly repeated grim spectacle had only succeeded in inspiring the naturally stubborn Hollanders with a determination to outmaneuver Spanish authorities in any and all ways possible, one of those being confrontation in the remote East.

When, in 1580, Philip II of Spain also became Philip I of Portugal, the Dutch future in the Far East was, without intention or planning, determined. In 1581, the northern Dutch provinces had joined together to declare themselves independent of Spain. Philip, who could tolerate heresy and the insubordination of subjects even less than his father, issued an edict that Dutch vessels, long accustomed to loading spice cargoes in Lisbon for distribution to more northerly European ports, were henceforth to be denied access to that port. Dutch ships then at anchor in Lisbon were confiscated. Thus Philip, who understood practically nothing of the Dutch mind, sent them scurrying towards the East, the original source of the forbidden cargoes.

All too aware of what Philip's Portuguese takeover might mean, the Dutch Cornelius van Houtman, who had been residing in Portugal first as a soldier then as a merchant, returned to his homeland to urge that the Dutch deal directly with the spice lands of the Far East. Houtman knew the route, having already sailed to the Far East on Portuguese expeditions. He now offered to put his knowledge and experience at the service of the newly independent Dutch, if they would pay the large fines that had been demanded in Lisbon of him and his brother. Houtman's offer was eagerly accepted. The little problem of maps and charts was quickly overcome

when a Dutch bookseller who had forehandedly managed to purchase twenty-five maps from a Spanish official
presented them to the Dutch government.

By 1595, a fleet of four ships, under Houtman, set
sail for the East via the Cape of Good Hope. Disaster
followed disaster and the voyage was successful only in
that it finally fixed the minds of Dutch navigators on the
need to learn more about the route east. Meanwhile, in
1596, Linschoten's travelogue was published. Within it,
along with his penetrating remarks on conditions in Goa,
he had added a supplementary manual for navigators in
which he described not only the route to be taken but
also currents, tradewinds, monsoons, harbors, shoals,
sunken rocks, and quicksands—in fact all the information which the Portuguese would not knowingly have
shared with a heretic from West Friesland. The Iberian
monopoly of the sea routes East was now broken. The
stage was now set for Dutch penetration of the East,
which was signalled by the founding of the "New Company" which, in 1598, was sending ships there.

So hungrily were the Dutch now eyeing the Far East
that they eagerly employed any skilled navigator who
came to their notice—a readiness in no way diminished
by Houtman's lack of real success. Thus, when the Earl
of Essex, serving in Holland with English forces sent
there by Queen Elizabeth I, recommended Captain John
Davis, just back from an Arctic voyage, the Dutch hastened to sign him up. In March 1598, he sailed from
Middleborough as pilot of a Dutch fleet. Back in Middleborough by August 1600, Davis sent a report to the
"Right Honourable, my exceeding good Lord and Master, Robert, Earle of Essex, etc." This suggests that the
earl had as an ulterior motive in recommending Davis,
the hope that Davis would come to know the sea lanes
of the East for the eventual benefit of England.

Davis's report to Essex runs, in part: "I have used
my best diligence to discharge my duty, as neere as my

slender capacitie could effect the same, according to those directions which your lordship gave mee in charge at my departure; when it pleased you to imploy mee in this Voyage, for the discovering of those Easterne parts of the world, to the service of her Majestie and the good of our Countrey. What I have seene I doe signifie in this Journall to your Lordship: and that which I have learned by the report of other Nations (when it shall please God to make me happie by your Lordships favourable presence), I will make farther knowne to your Lordship, as well of the King of Portugall his places of Trade, as the enterchangeable trading of those Easterne Nations among themselves."[3] After listing places and peoples visited, Davis closes his report with more than a hint that some recompense is now due him. It certainly seems to have been but perhaps earls were no more generous than kings in their manner of showing gratitude.

All in all, 1600 was an exciting year for Dutch maritime enterprises. A few months after Davis's departure, another expedition, fitted out by private enterprise, was undertaken to reach the South Sea and beyond by way of Magellan's Straits. It was to be a disastrous voyage, making Dutch sponsors unhappily aware that decisions as to the exact route to be followed should not be made by people remaining at home, some of whom may never themselves have navigated the great oceans, but left that to the men who were voyaging.

With Admiral Jacob Mahu in command, the expedition left Holland in June 1598, under instructions to head down the coast of Africa before crossing the Atlantic towards the straits. Off the African coast, delayed by the usual unpredictable weather of that region, many of the crew sickened with fever, the admiral himself died. As a consequence, the fleet of seven ships did not reach the South American coast before April 1599. Five months later, they emerged from the cold, stormy, treacherous straits to face a scarcely more hospitable ocean.

At some point on the land near their exit from the straits, the crews of those seven ships, now led by Admiral de Cordes, gathered to raise a memorial to themselves, the Netherlanders who had been the first to take a fleet of "heavy" ships through those straits. In commemoration of this event, they there founded a new order of knighthood—the Knights of the Unchained Lion, of which the fleet's chief officers were knights-commanders and the most deserving men of the crews knights-brethren. All joined in vowing that "by no danger, no necessity, nor by the fear of death, would they ever be moved to undertake anything prejudicial to their honor, to the welfare of the fatherland, or to the success of the enterprise in which they were engaged; pledging themselves to stake their lives in order, consistently with their honor, to inflict every possible damage on the hereditary enemy, and to plant the banner of Holland in those territories whence the King of Spain gathered the treasures with which he carried on his perpetual war against the Netherlands."[4] Never having known real peace during their lifetimes, these Hollanders meant every word of the fierce vows they were taking before leaving behind the Spanish-claimed soil of Patagonia.

The particular king of Spain who inspired those vows—Philip II—was already dead, though the new knights would not learn of his death for a long time to come. However, neither Philip nor his successor could have perceived menace in vows taken by a small group of dissident subjects gathered in a remote land which he claimed by papal decree. The stubborn determination of the newly independent Dutch provinces was something such kings must learn the hard way.

Disaster upon disaster followed the Dutch expedition, one ship after another disappearing, to be heard of no more. Of the original seven, only one ever returned to Holland. Another reached Japan where, although the crew fell into hostile hands, a great trade between the two lands was begun. Yet another ship reached a far southern island group, possibly today's South Shetlands, before the voyage came to an end.

By 1602, as the historian of the Netherlands wrote:

> The same fishermen and fighting men, whom we have but lately seen sailing forth from Zeeland and Friesland to confront the dangers of either pole, were now contending in the Indian seas with the Portuguese monopolists of the tropics.
>
> A century long, the generosity of the Roman pontiff in bestowing upon others what was not his property had guaranteed to the nation of Vasco da Gama one half at least of the valuable possessions which maritime genius, unflinching valour, and boundless cruelty had won and kept. But the spirit of change was abroad in the world. Potentates and merchants under the equator had been sedulously taught that there were no other white men on the planet but the Portuguese and their conquerors the Spaniards, and that the Dutch . . . were a mere mob of pirates inhabiting the obscurest of dens. . . .
>
> Early in this year Andreas Hurtado de Mendoza with a stately fleet of galleons and smaller vessels, more than five-and-twenty in all, was on his way toward the island of Java to inflict summary vengeance upon those oriental rulers who had dared to trade with men forbidden by his Catholic Majesty and the Pope.[5]

Headed for Bantam (not far from today's Djakarta), Mendoza reached there while a Dutch skipper named Wolfert Hermann, in command of five small trading vessels in which there were about 300 men, arrived to continue the illicit Dutch commerce. Hermann's "whole force of both men and guns was far inferior to the flagship alone of Mendoza." But he determined to demonstrate that the Dutch were not about to give up their trade nor desert "their newly found friends in the hour of danger. To the profound astonishment of the Portuguese admiral, the Dutchman with his five little trading ships made an attack on the pompous armada, intending to avert chastisement from the king of Batavia." Avoiding close quarters with the superior forces, Hermann used his nautical skills as well as the greater maneuverability of his little trading vessels to circle round and round the "ponderous, much-puzzled Portuguese fleet, until by well-directed shots and skilful manoeuvering they had sunk several ships, taken two, run others into the shallows and, at last, put the whole to confusion."[6] Thus foiled by the skill and audacity of his insignificant opponent, the Portuguese admiral turned his back on the Dutch and bore away with what was left of his fleet for the island of Amboina, nearly 1500 miles to the east, where he laid waste several villages together with their surrounding spice plantations, achieving thereby only an increase in the hostility already felt by local peoples toward the Portuguese.

The victorious Dutch, having by their demonstration of naval prowess earned the respect of local rulers, sailed on from island to island, reaching Banda, not far from Amboina, where nutmegs and cloves served as the chief articles of exchange. Among these islands, Hermann made treaties with the rulers, specifying that none but the Dutch should henceforth be permitted to purchase their spices and that neither nation should give aid to refugees from the other. These provisions were specifically designed to clip the wings of the Portuguese who had previously claimed monopoly of the spice trade while insisting that their rivals, the Dutch, came from low dens of robbers. To counteract this carefully planted notion, Hermann took home with him from Sumatra official envoys who, it was planned, should learn first-hand and report on the kinds of thriving cities the ignorant Portuguese considered robbers' dens.

In the course of the voyage home, Hermann had a splendid opportunity to demonstrate to his oriental passengers how well able he and his countrymen might be to protect their homelands from Portuguese attacks. Encountering a richly laden homeward-bound Portuguese carrack, he attacked and overpowered her much as he had Mendoza's fleet off Bantam. Then, having divided the booty between officers and crews in the then customary manner, he set the Portuguese crew safely on shore at St. Helena and wended his triumphant way home, reaching there in 1602.

The Dutch had not been waiting for Hermann's return to undertake new voyages to the East. Other captains had been busily making treaties of their own with various spice islands. One Captain Nek extended his voyage to include Ceylon whose chief exportable product was cinnamon. Captain Jakob Heemskerk, recently returned from that miserable polar winter spent on Novaya Zemlya, was now warming himself along the coast of India, pushing as far east as the coast of China in command of two small galleons and crews totaling not more than 130 men. When he encountered, in the Straits of Malacca, a great Lisbon carrack "laden with pearls, spices, brocades and precious stones, on its way to Europe," the commander who had not shrunk from single-handed encounter with a polar bear, did not now hesitate to attack the thousand-tun, seventeen-gun carrack and "after a combat of but brief duration, Heemskerk was master of the carrack. He spared the lives of his 700 prisoners, and set them on shore before they should have time to discover to what a handful of Dutchmen they had surrendered."[7]

Such legendary encounters and the visible riches they had diverted from Portuguese pockets delighted ordinary Hollanders. The merchants who had underwritten the voyages and made the fortunes were not quite so easy in their minds. There were dangers in the rivalry that was springing up between the various towns whence the fleets had sailed—dangers which were increased when the rivalries were extended to oriental ports. Such independent voyages, no matter how immediately successful, could add up to disaster.

"Merchants arriving at the different Indian ports would often find that their own countrymen had been too quick for them . . . that the eastern markets had been stripped, and that prices had gone up to a ruinous height, while on the other hand, in the Dutch cities, nutmegs and sinnamon, brocades and indigo were as plentiful as red herrings." That free competition and individual enterprise, which had been enriching Hollanders and Javanese respectively with a superfluity of purchasable commodities, "seemed likely to end in general catastrophe."[8]

To ward off that catastrophe, the States General of the Netherlands granted a charter to a single great company with what, for those times, was an enormous paid-up capital. All former trading companies were invited—the invitation not being of a kind that could be declined—to merge themselves in the Universal East India Company which, for twenty-one years, should alone have the right to trade to the east of the Cape of Good Hope and to sail through the Straits of Magellan. The charter, renewable after each period of twenty-one years, was signed on 20 March 1602. The chambers of Amsterdam, Zeeland, Delft, Rotterdam, Enkhuizen, and Hoorn were, according to the financial investment of each, to govern the Universal Company which was granted the right to make treaties with Indian powers in the name of the States General of the United Netherlands, build fortresses, appoint generals, and levy troops which then must take oaths of fidelity to the States and

to the Company.[9] "No ships, artillery, or other muni-
tions of war belonging to the Company were to be used
in the service of the country without permission of the
Company." The admiralty was assigned a certain share
of such prizes as were conquered from the enemy—the
enemy, of course, being Portugal or Spain, whose carracks the admiralty might find useful. In short, like the
English East India Company founded two years earlier,
the Dutch Company was a super-state, to become by
1621 *Vereenigde Oost-Indische Compagnie*, referred to as
VOC. Both companies would grow in power and arrogance until they won themselves as many enemies in the
Far East as had the Portuguese and Spanish in their time,
and by so doing bring their dominance there to an end.

Meanwhile, the Dutch commercial corporation thus
organized intended, at all costs, to keep a firm hold on
trade in Eastern commodities and all that such a trade
might involve. Any and all other European traders, including Dutch individualists, must bow to the company's power and obey its edicts. Governors of the Dutch
East Indies, under the company of course, were presently reigning with a power no less great and far more
extensive than that of the Oriental potentates whom
they were, for all practical purposes, replacing. Any
supposedly offending and offended Dutchman had the
right to appeal his case to authorities in Holland—which
privilege demanded that the offender should live long
enough and have ample funds to live on until his case
was decided.

The company's officials believed that its monopoly
was clinched through the fact that passage to the East
by both the Cape of Good Hope route and that of
Magellan's Straits was sternly interdicted for all but
company ships—an interdiction which would be actively
enforced by those formidable fleets of the states and of
the company. The almost universal assumption was that
those two routes were the only possible ones for passing

from the South Atlantic into any part of the South Sea. That any navigator might not share that assumption or, rejecting it, might have the courage and funds to seek out another passage, was not a thought which occurred to the monopolists any more than, in Magellan's day, the existence of his straits had been believable to the Portuguese king and his advisors.

The year 1619, however, saw the publication in England of the translation of a Dutch book, written within the two previous years and titled, in part, *A Voyage Around the World by a New Passage*. The translator, "W.P."—probably one William Philip—dedicated his translation to the director of the English East India Company, founded in 1600 under a charter of Queen Elizabeth I. As translator W. Philip understood only too well, the subject dealt with was bound to be of the greatest interest to the director of the English company.

> The generall States of the United Netherland-Provinces, having granted their Letters Patent to the East India Company resident in the sayd Provinces, to trafficke in the Indies, and none other but they onely, with a stricke prohibition unto all other Marchants, and inhabitants of the sayd Countries, not to sayle or trafficke Eastward beyond the Cape de bona esperance, nor through the Straits of Magellan westward, either into India, or any other unknowne or not discovered countries, Isaak le Maire, a rich Marchant of Amsterdam, dwelling in Egmont, having a great desire to trafficke into strange and farre Countries, and William Cornelison Schouten of Horne (a man well experienced in Seafaring, who before that time had sayled thrice into most partes of the East Indies, for Maister, Pilot, and Marchant) and yet very desirous to sayle into and discover new and

unknown Countries, oftentimes speaking and conferring together, reasoned among themselves, whether they might not enter into the great South Sea by another way (then through the same wayes which in the East India Companies Letters Pattens are formerly forbidden and prohibited).[10]

Having thus conferred and reasoned, Lemaire and Schouten began putting their thoughts into action with typical Dutch energy and thoroughness. They secured two ships whose names, *Hoorn* and *Eendracht*, were reported in English as *Horne* and *Unitie*, had them outfitted, manned, and ready to sail by 14 June 1615. Within six months, while she was being careened somewhere along the coast of Patagonia, the *Eendracht* caught fire and had to be abandoned. The *Hoorn* kept on with the voyage as planned and, on 29 January following "about evening we saw land againe lying northwest and north northwest from us, which was the land that lay south from the straights of Magellan, which reacheth Southward, all high hillie land covered over with snow, ending in a sharp pointe, which we called Cape Horne"[11]—not because of the shape of the promontory but after both the discovering ship and the city from which she had come.

About three days later, Schouten was convinced that they had already entered the South Sea but it was not until nearly two more weeks had passed that they dared to celebrate: "The 12. our men had each three cups of wine in signe of joy for our good hap, for then the Streightes of *Magellan* lay east from us."[12] The same day they named the passage just discovered by them the "Straights of Le Maire," a name which still remains on the maps, as also do "Cape Horn" and the far southern "Staten Islands," so named in honor of the States General.

For some years, the States General would regard that as a doubtful honor. When the *Hoorn* reached the Dutch East Indies after a ten-month crossing of the Pacific, no one there would believe the ship had not come by a forbidden passage. The "unchained lion" in the person of the hard-bitten Dutch governor-general roared loudly. Ship and wares were seized, the owners sent home to Holland as prisoners after the governor had sternly told them that if they believed they had been wronged, "they should right themselves in Holland." Two years later the High Court in Holland declared in their favor but meanwhile LeMaire had died on the voyage home, his son already dead in the Indies. Only Schouten remained to taste the triumph the voyage of his *Hoorn* had earned—and, fortunately, to leave a record of that voyage.

Meanwhile, the Dutch in the East were losing no time in making good the vows, taken at the exit from Magellan's straits by the Knights of the Unchained Lion—"to inflict every possible damage on the hereditary enemy, and to plant the banner of Holland in those territories whence the King of Spain gathered the treasures with which he carried on his perpetual war against the Netherlands."[13] "Planting the banner" was a euphemism for a Far Eastern war as unremitting as the one the king of Spain had been carrying on against European heretics. The feisty Dutch were prepared to fight to the death to take over any and all Eastern lands to which Spain and Portugal laid claim. The Dutch soldiers and sailors had the advantage of their foes in that they knew exactly what they were fighting for—the exercise of their reformed religion and the independence of the land of their birth. The Spanish and Portuguese forces, on the other hand, were fighting for no particular principle but for a remote royal figure none could know personally and some were even beginning to resent. Both sides, of course, had a large share of men who believed that victory might produce the riches in spices and oriental fabrics to parlay into large personal fortunes.

Meanwhile, they dug in. In 1619, near the northern tip of Java and perhaps fifty miles from the native town of Bantam, the Dutch East India Company founded its own capital, and named it Batavia after their homeland. Today it has become Djakarta. Like the Dutch homeland, Batavia was wet almost to the point of swampiness but, unlike Holland, it was, as the Dutch captain Stavorinus was to call it a century and a half later, "one of the unwholesomest spots on the face of the globe," where "the destructive unhealthiness of the climate is carried to the very pinnacle of corruption."[14] In this "unwholesome" spot, the Dutch East India Company centered the power it exercised over the lands of Southeast Asia including the fertile, if only slightly less unhealthy, islands.

Having set themselves the task of driving the Spanish king's subjects out of their Eastern strongholds and putting the control of shipping and cargoes there in official Dutch hands, the company's people set about it with a will. It helped in the beginning that Eastern potentates, tired of the demands of their Latin adversaries and masters, welcomed the Dutch. A time for disillusionment would come but in the meanwhile these potentates were enjoying the spectacle of Portuguese being forced to give up lands they had long claimed. Both sides in this struggle depended in part on the services of local fighting men and thus, inevitably, both had to contend with the greed and treachery of mercenaries.

Reaching out far toward the east, the Dutch established a Formosan station by 1625. In 1641 they captured Malacca, on the Malay Peninsula, from the Portuguese. Ceylon, of which Pyrard de Laval had once written, "no words can describe the goodness, richness, and fertility of this island," and its valuable cinnamon crops had been taken over by the Dutch by 1656. The Portuguese were entirely driven out, as they would, bit by bit, be driven out of all their Eastern strongholds save Goa and Macao, which survived as Portuguese enclaves into the twentieth century.

Meanwhile, the Dutch company was contending with the English for domination of the Spice Islands and of the spice-rich Malay archipelago. All of this was being undertaken by a land not materially larger or wealthier than Portugal which until then had dominated Far Eastern commerce, not only for voyages to and from the homeland but for those of the Eastern coasting trade. At the zenith of its power in 1669, the Dutch East India Company owned 150 trading ships, 40 ships of war, employed 10,000 soldiers and paid a dividend of 40 percent.

The Dutch had profited by the sea routes and trade monopolies they seized from the Portuguese but sadly failed to profit by the lessons they might have learned by studying the rise and fall of Portuguese power in the East, by assessing Portuguese relationships with native rulers and their people, and by reminding themselves what their own presence there might have suggested— that yet other European lands would reach out to seize their piece of the spicy pie.

13

The Queen's Avenger

The English, no less than the Dutch, had good reason for resenting the expanding Spanish empire, though in England's case this resentment was epitomized in a personal antagonism between the English and Spanish monarchs. Elizabeth I had good reason for annoyance at Philip's pretensions. She saw those fortunes in Far Eastern spices and other commodities, as well as the gold and silver pouring into his coffers from the Americas, as the means of financing his unremitting wars against England and other heretical lands. The tables could neatly be turned against Philip if those fortunes could be channeled into the coffers of the lands he was bent on subjugating. The queen had felt a moral obligation to send token forces under Essex to aid the heretic Dutch. Yet she could not be unaware that those same Dutch might presently become England's rivals. England could use those Far Eastern riches, too, and England had the means, as yet untested in a critical encounter, to seize some for herself.

For Elizabeth, those means were her skilled mariners, as bold and brave as were the Dutch, who would take English ships into seas over which Spain claimed dominion. It would supply added motivation if the mariners happened to have some personal grudge against Spain and the Spaniards. Whom it was she first consulted in this matter, who suggested the names of likely mariners, remains a state secret although her secretary of state, Robert Walsingham, may well have had a hand in suggesting Francis Drake.

Drake, a swashbuckling son of the age, was already known to be a skilled navigator, as well as a confirmed Philip-hater because of the treachery encountered by himself and John Hawkins. This occurred during the late 1560s, when Hawkins' West Indian fleet had dropped anchor at San Juan de Ullua (today's Veracruz, Mexico) after having received a safe-conduct from the viceroy. The safe-conduct was worthless, the ships attacked, the crews seized, then handed over to the Inquisition to be questioned, tortured, and burned alive. Drake and Hawkins managed to make their escape, taking with them an inextinguishable hatred of all things Spanish—a hatred that remained active during the following decade while Drake was cruising the Caribbean as a privateer, at one and the same time seizing rich booty and paying off a personal score. When, in the course of that voyage, he marched across the isthmus of Panama and on the far side climbed a tree that gave him his first view of the great Pacific Ocean, he promised himself that he should be the first Englishman to sail that sea in an English bottom—most certainly to the detriment of Spain and her colonies.

Back home in England, during an audience with his queen, Drake made it pretty clear where his own thoughts and ambitions were tending. Avoiding an open avowal of her own inextinguishable hostility to Philip, Elizabeth murmured, "Drake, so it is that I would gladly be avenged upon the king of Spain for divers injuries

that I have received."[1] Exactly what the three of them—
the queen, Walsingham, and Drake—decided upon in
private conclave is not now known, but by November
1577, "by gracious commission from his soveraigne, and
with the helpe of divers friends adventurers, he had
fitted himself with five ships."[2] The queen was giving
the proposed voyage no more than her unofficial blessing, having cautioned Drake, "Fail not lest I disavow the
lot o' ye."[3] Thus, when later derogatory remarks were
being made and the Spanish ambassador was pressing to
have Drake disowned and Philip reimbursed for Drake's
freebooting, she could shrug her shoulders and murmur,
"The gentleman careth not if I disown him."[4]

Aware that the success of his proposed voyage might
depend upon the grandness of the impression he could
make on peoples of far lands, Drake equipped the
"hundred-tonne admirall" the *Pelican* (presently to be
renamed the *Golden Hind*) with articles that could adver-
tise his importance. Reverend Francis Fletcher, journal-
ist of the voyage, described this equipping: "These ships
he mand with 164. able and sufficient men, and furnished them also with such plentifull provision of all
things necessary. . . . Neither had he omitted, to make
provision also for ornament and delight, carrying to this
purpose with him, expert musicians, rich furniture (all
the vessels for his table, yea many belonging even to the
Cooke-roome being of pure silver) and divers shewes of
all sorts of curious workmanship, whereby the civilitie
and magnificence of his native countrie, might, among
all nations whithersoever he should come, be the more
admired."[5]

If Spanish galleons were not to lie in wait and
intercept the fleet before it reached the Pacific, secrecy
had to be maintained. None of the 164 men in Drake's
fleet were told beforehand where he was heading. All
somehow believed that Alexandria, Egypt, was to be
their destination and they were still believing that for

several weeks after setting sail. The voyage seemed to go smoothly enough though there was some undercurrent of complaint which would come to a head after they reached Patagonia in June 1578. There, in Port St. Julian, with its grim reminders of the mutineers who had almost destroyed Magellan's voyage of fifty years before, Drake, too, had to quell a threatened mutiny planned by a man who Drake, in spite of prior warnings, had believed to be his friend—the vice-admiral of the fleet, Thomas Doughty.

Even though he held the queen's commission, Drake knew himself to be in a ticklish position which might prove fatal should the aging queen die before his return. The queen's chief minister, Burghley, had been against the voyage and the challenge to Spain it implied. Could Burghley have expressed himself in a way that encouraged Doughty's ambitions? This made Doughty a dangerous companion. It was, for Drake, a situation that demanded both tact and decisiveness.

Fletcher, having recorded the initial hostility of the Patagonians, continued his narrative, "To this evill, thus received at the hands of the infidells, there was adjoined, and grew another mischief, wrought and contrived closely amongst our selves, as great, yea farre greater and of farre more greivous consequence then the former: but that it was by Gods providence detected and prevented in time." He outlined the plot against the voyage and against the person of Drake. "These plotts," Fletcher continued, "had been layd before the voyage beganne in England: the very modell of them was shewed, and declared to our generall in his garden at Plimouth, before his setting sayle."[6] If Drake then believed the accusations against a man whom he regarded as a friend, he may have convinced himself that he could wean Doughty from his plans in the course of the voyage.

"But at length," Fletcher explained, "perceiving that his lenity and favours did little good; in that the heat of ambition was not yet allayed, nor could be quenched, as it seemed, but by blood . . . he thought it high time, to call these practices into question, before it was too late to call any question of them into hearing. And therefore setting good watch over him, and assembling all his Captaines, and gentlemen of his company together,"[7] he laid the evidence before them and asked that they be the judges. The verdict was unanimous—"Guilty!"—upon which the guilty party was given a choice between being left behind in Patagonia, being sent home in disgrace, or immediate execution. Considering immediate death to be preferable to death among savages or public disgrace at home, Doughty chose execution.

The little fleet of six vessels was now reduced to three, "that we might easier keepe our selves together, be the better furnished with necessaries, and be the stronger against whatsoever need should be."[8] By 20 August they were about to enter the straits and there Drake is said to have taken on himself Francis Fletcher's duty and preached a sermon that has outlived any delivered by the fleet's pastor, the most memorable phrases being, "I must have the gentlemen to haul and draw with the mariner and the mariner with the gentlemen. . . . I would know him that would refuse to set his hand to a rope."[9] Here was a formula for survival that might have helped keep afloat many a doomed carrack, overloaded as such usually were with Spanish and Portuguese gentlemen and their servants, all overly fastidious in matters of manual labor if not of personal cleanliness. At that same ceremony and with a flourish of trumpets, Drake changed the name of his ship from the *Pelican* to the more romantic-sounding *Golden Hind*.

The dangerous and winding straits were entered, but in spite of typically violent contrary winds, sixteen days later Drake reached the South Sea, "called by some *Mare Pacificum*, but proving rather to be *Mare furiosum*."[10]

The same passage had taken Magellan thirty-seven days and was, a decade after Drake, to take his fellow countryman Cavendish forty-nine days. Drake's fleet was in the Pacific soon reduced to a single ship, the 100- to 120-ton *Golden Hind*, the "Vice-admirall" *Elizabeth* (80 tons) having given up and returned home after exhausting efforts to buck the headwinds at the straits' exit. The little *Marigold* (30 tons) simply disappeared with all hands on board.

The "Generall," as Fletcher referred to Drake, was a fascinating combination of schoolboy prankster and mature and vengeful mariner. The *Golden Hind*'s voyage up the west coast of South America reads something like that of a seagoing Till Eulenspiegel, who was supposed to have enlivened the medieval world with his pranks. Francis Fletcher, despite his "reverend" status, was of a temperament that delighted in the fun and games which he duly and typically reported: "The next harbor therefore which we chanced with on April 15. in 15.deg. 40.min. was Guatulco so named of the inhabitants who inhabited it, with whom we had some entercourse, to the supply of many things which we desired, and chiefly bread &c. and now having reasonably, as we thought, provided our selves, we departed from the coast of America for the present: but not forgetting, before we gate a-shipboard, to take with us also a certaine pot (of about a bushell in bignesse) full of ryalls of plate, which we found in town: together with a chaine of gold, and some other jewels, which we intreated a gentleman Spaniard to leave behinde him, as he was flying out of towne."[11]

Curiously, Hakluyt's *Principal Navigations* also gives a report of this episode but from the point of view of the Englishman John Chilton who was in New Spain trading for cotton and that precious blue plant-produced dystuff, indigo. At "a port in the South Sea, called Aquitula . . . Sir Francis Drake arrived in the yeare 1579 in the moneth of April, where I lost with his being there about 1000 duckets which he took away, with some other goods of other merchants of Mexico, from one Francisco Gomes Rangifa, factor there for all the Spanish merchants that then traded in the South Sea."[12]

Being not only a superior navigator but also a man of unswervable determination, Drake never thought of giving up his voyage even after the disappearance of the *Marigold* left the *Golden Hind* (only about two-thirds the tonnage of the future *Mayflower*) the sole survivor of his fleet. He made his way north, surprising and raiding one coastal settlement after another, as in his visit to "Guatulco," or "Aquitula" (both probably refer to today's Acapulco). He made a point of treating well the Spaniards he captured, releasing them unharmed, undoubtedly after having pumped them dry of any possible information as to treasure to be collected on his voyage north as well as routes towards the Spice Islands.

If a prisoner happened to be a Spaniard of rank against whom Drake had no personal grudge, he was treated with ceremony, entertained at the captain's table, with musical accompaniment, and eventually released with his personal property more or less intact. One such prisoner, Don Francisco de Zárate, later reported to the viceroy—the very one who, six years earlier at San Juan de Ullua, had earned Drake's undying hatred—that Drake, surrounded with all possible pomp and circumstance, "dines and sups to the music of viols. He carries trained carpenters and artisans, so as to be able to careen the ship at any time." Drake, Zárate reported, was "about thirty-five years of age, low of stature, with a fair beard, and is one of the greatest mariners that sail the seas, both as navigator and as a commander. . . . I managed to ascertain that the General was well liked, and all said they adored him."[13]

One can imagine the viceroy, on reading this report, gnashing his teeth in rage for having permitted the vile, piratical heretic to escape. Worse still, the escaped prisoner had managed to surround himself with luxury and to win the respect and admiration of subordinates as well as (perish the thought!) of Don Francisco de Zárate. All this was achieved with a ship of a size altogether negligible compared to Spain's great carracks, and manned by less than sixty men. Some of these, incidentally, must have doubled as the servants who had so ceremoniously waited on their captain and his guests. It was a scene that could have appealed to the age's popular playwrights, William Shakespeare or Miguel Cervantes.

One of the most valuable bits of Drake's booty— more valuable even than all the treasure collected in coastal settlements or from coasting carracks—was a set of charts and sailing directions for crossing the South Sea. Drake was determined to do this in spite of all the viceroy's efforts to see to it that the heretic should not again escape his clutches. Neatly eluding all pursuers, Drake arrived in late June 1579 at some point along the California coast where he spent about five weeks resting and having the *Golden Hind* put in readiness for the demanding transpacific voyage.

Drake must also have toyed with the idea of enhancing his reputation by discovering the elusive northwest passage. Before he landed in California he had sailed north along the coast to about 48° North, but the westward trend of the coast plus the increasingly chilly air— especially so for men who had recently been passing through the tropics—must have persuaded him that no such passage existed or that if there was one, navigation through it could not be practicable.

Having reached this decision, Drake set out to follow the usual route (for Spaniards at least) across the Pacific, to arrive at the Ladrones after sixty-eight days sailing. By early November, he had reached the Spice Islands, where he soon was made aware of local political undercurrents. "These are foure high piked Ilands," wrote Francis Fletcher. "Their names Tírenate, Tídore, Matchan, Batchan, all of them very fruitfull, and yeelding abundance of cloves. . . . At the East of them lyes a very great Iland called Gillola."[14]

Ternate's king soon contacted the new arrivals through a representative who cautioned them to avoid Tidore and do all their business with Ternate's king. Drake was assured that

> he should find that he was a king, his word should stand; whereas if he dealt with the Portingals [who controlled Tidore] he should find in them nothing but deceit and treachery. And besides that if he went to Tidore before he came to Terenate, then would his king have nothing to do with us, for he held the Portingall as an enemy. On these persuasions our Generall resolved to runne with Terenate, where the next day very early in the morning we came to anchor: And presently our Generall sent a messenger to the king with a velvet cloake, for a present and as a token that his coming should be in peace: and that he required no other thing at his hands, but that (his victuals being spent in so long a voiage) he might have supply from him by way of traffique and exchange of merchandise (whereof he had a store of divers sorts) of such things as he wanted.[15]

Presently the *Golden Hind* was receiving "what was there to be had, by way of traffique, to wit, rice in pretty quantity, hennes, sugar canes, imperfect and liquid sugar, a fruit which they call *Figo* (*Magellane* calls it figge of a span long, but is no other than that which the Spaniards and Portingalls have named *Plantanes*")—and which we today call bananas. "Cocoes and a kind of meale which they call *Sago* . . . for a few cloves wee did also traffique, whereof for a small matter, wee might have had greater store, then we could well tell where to bestow: but our generall's care was, that the ship should not be too much pestered or annoyed therewith."[16]

To the Portuguese in those islands, it all constituted an intrusion which they would neither forgive nor forget. Four years later, a young English merchant named John Newberie, who with three companions had reached Ormuz (opposite the southeasternmost point of Arabia), was imprisoned there by the Portuguese and presently transferred south to Goa. Newberie wrote from Goa: "There were two causes which moved the Captaines of Ormuz to imprison us & afterward send us hither"—the first cause being false accusations made by a rival Italian merchant, and "the second was that M. Drake at his being at Maluco, caused two pieces of his ordinance to be shot at a gallion of the kinges of Portingall, as they say . . . and amongst the rest he said that M. Drake was sent out of England with many shippes, and came to Maluco, and laded cloves"[17]—by all odds the more serious offense of the two. It had taken four years for the *Golden Hind* to multiply into a fleet of "many shippes" and her token spice cargo to become lading for that fleet. Thus are legends born, especially when the man involved was of legendary quality!

Mariner before he was merchant, Drake had firmly suppressed all temptation to overload the *Golden Hind* with precious spices. By the time he reached the Moluccas, she was already loaded practically to the limit of safety with the heavy captured Spanish treasure. Cloves were in a quite different category than such Far Eastern commodities as jewels and brocades. Any intelligent captain would know that what a ship failed to load one year could be replaced by another year's crop of the plant product. The main thing was to reach England safely and alert other English mariners to try their own luck on the far side of the globe.

"Safely" was the key word and for Drake it meant

more than just being able to drop anchor off Plymouth. His awareness of this is shown in the first question he asked of the man who greeted him on his arrival—did Her Majesty still enjoy good health? Drake knew only too well that if she had died during his absence, his moment of triumph might turn into disaster and he even find himself condemned as a pirate rather than acclaimed a national hero.

The voyage had been notable in more ways than one. In addition to Drake's being the first Englishman to complete a circumnavigation, he had, after more than three years' absence, brought the *Golden Hind* home with the loss of no more than seventeen men—not so much by disease and starvation, as had been so common in Portuguese and Spanish ships, but by accidents or encounters with Patagonians and Spanish. It was a remarkable record, not to be outdone for a couple of centuries after.

The actual value of the plunder Drake delivered to the Tower of London (and other strongholds where there was less likelihood of spies toting up the whole) has never been determined for certain. It has been variously estimated, even to as much as a million pounds. Whatever the actual total turned out to be, Elizabeth graciously permitted Francis Drake to retain 10,000 pounds for himself, in addition to having him knighted on the deck of his *Golden Hind*. The merchant-adventurers who had underwritten the voyage were said to have profited to the tune of 1000 percent on their investments. Of course, the Spanish ambassador in London fumed, making every possible effort to persuade the queen to repudiate Drake and turn his loot over to Spain. When she firmly rejected that suggestion, she set in motion the events which were, less than a decade later, to culminate in the sailing of the Spanish Armada and a conflict in which Drake played a more-than-willing part. In the end, Drake was defeated by yellow fever, dying in 1596 at Nombre de Diós, Panamá. He was buried at sea, to become a legendary hero in England and in Spain, the notorious *El Draque* which Spanish mothers long used to frighten naughty children into obedience.

The second Englishman, and the third mariner of any nation, to circumnavigate the globe was that "worshipful and worthy gentleman, Master Thomas Candish," since referred to as Thomas Cavendish. Having acquired and outfitted three ships—the *Desire*, the largest, being of about the same tonnage as Drake's *Golden Hind*, the *Content* of about half that tonnage, and the *Hugh Gallant*, a mere third—Cavendish set sail in June 1586, to arrive off the "Cape of California" by October 1587. There he lay in wait for the Manila galleon, captured it, and transferred to his own fleet no more than "fortie tunnes of the chiefest merchandise." He then set the galleon and its remaining contents on fire. The Spanish prisoners were set on shore unharmed, unless one counts the long journey on foot that they had to make to reach Mexican settlements. For Cavendish, as well as for Drake, the powerful motivating force had been active antagonism to the king of Spain and to his Church. "In this voyage," Cavendish reported gleefully, "we burnt twentie sayles of Spanish shippes, besides divers of their Townes and Villages."[18]

Thereafter, Cavendish made the usual Pacific crossing, stopping by the Ladrones, Philippines and Moluccas, to arrive back in England on 9 September 1588, a mere two months after the destruction of the Spanish Armada had left England free to aspire to the position of mistress of the seas. However, this did not mean that English mariners might now enjoy undisputed access to lands in distant seas but that England had put herself in a position to challenge, with reasonable expectation of success, other claims to exclusive dominion over such lands, the routes that led to them, and, most important, over their commodities.

The English merchant-adventurers who had already risked so much, and sometimes won so much, in sponsoring voyages, became alarmed as they watched practical monopoly of the European spice trade gradually pass from Portuguese control to that of the more thoroughly mercantile Dutch. The price of pepper had already risen sharply from three to eight shillings per pound and no one knew how much higher it would go unless something was done to stem the Dutch tide in some manner short of war. To achieve this, the English merchants knew that they must suppress their own rivalries and combine their efforts as the Dutch were already doing and would make official by 1602.

Merchant Robert Thorne's report, which had long before encouraged mariners to attempt a shorter northern passage to the Orient, had also underlined the great wealth that Far Eastern trade was bringing to the coffers of the king of Portugal and of Spain. English merchants had been dreaming of investing in expeditions to the Far East—and now, after the Armada's defeat, this became a real possibility.

To this end, they proposed to purchase ships, engage mariners and send them forth with the moral, if not financial support of the sovereign. The queen was easily persuaded of the advantages in an organized effort and, by the last day of the last month of the sixteenth century, granted a Charter of Incorporation to "The Governor and Company of Merchants of London trading into the East Indies." The East India Company, as it soon became known (and popularly baptized the "John Company") was to have, for fifteen years, the exclusive right to trade with all countries lying beyond the Cape of Good Hope and the Straits of Magellan—if it could enforce that right, of course. Interlopers, homegrown as well as foreign, would risk forfeiture of ships and cargoes, if and when caught. It was the same old formula in new language.

For those who had cannily subscribed, the East Indian trade was soon bringing profits of 100 percent, so that even before the first fifteen years were up, the company's charter was renewed by King James I, in 1609. This renewal was "for ever" though with the proviso that should profits decline, the charter might be revoked on three years' notice.

Well before they received the Charter of Incorporation, promoters of the company had been busily planning their first fleet. Having purchased and equipped ships, they looked around for pilots who already knew their way east. But where were such to be found? Cavendish had died in 1591, Drake in 1596. Most other skilled pilots were of unacceptable nationalities. There remained, however, one Englishman who had won fame through northern voyages and who also had taken a ship to the East, though in Dutch employ. This was John Davis, who was easily persuaded to accept the post of pilot major of the first East India Company fleet which was made up of five ships which sailed for the East in mid-February 1600, to return by mid-September 1603. During the following year, Davis again sailed for the company, apparently under orders to pursue trade as far east as China and Japan. In December 1605, however, the fleet had an encounter with Japanese pirates in which Davis was killed.

Meanwhile, other English mariners had had a chance to become familiar with the sea routes to the East. Nothing would now stop the company from sending out regular, approximately annual fleets. Nothing, for that matter, was to stop the Dutch either.

14

John Company vs. Jan Compagnie

Having duly received the blessing of and perhaps some financial backing from his own king, any European navigator who undertook to search out new and remote lands was sure to carry with him a letter of greeting from the sponsoring monarch to whatever distant ruler might be encountered. That such a message, even if skillfully translated, might yet convey little meaning to men of alien lands, was not then perceived. A monarch was a monarch, his word law in his own land, his friendship, coveted by monarchs of other lands, to be wooed by flattering words and dazzling gifts.

For the native potentates the big question, unresolved by flattering words, was what really made those strange men in great and fearsome ships suddenly appear in their harbors. To the Zamorin of Calicut, as well as to his courtiers, there could be only one of two reasons: conquest or trade. Since it then appeared that the new arrivals were not bent on conquest, it must be trade as it had long been with the Arabs who regularly arrived in dhows or by caravan. Somewhat encouraged by the possibility that here, at last, might be rivals to the pushing Arabs who had so dominated trade in Calicut, the Zamorin had sent an appropriate message back to Portugal via da Gama's returning fleet. The significant part of this message to the king of Portugal ran: "In my kingdom, there is abundance of cinnamon, cloves, ginger, pepper, and precious stones. What I seek from thy country is gold, silver, coral, and scarlet"—obviously to underwrite his luxurious life style.

Clearly, the Zamorin saw this new kind of merchant as a variant on those who had for centuries been coming and going on the Malabar coast. He thought he knew how to handle merchants to his own profit, never dreaming that this kind of merchant might come to stay, and that others might follow to transfer deepseated European rivalries to the East. The grim potential, even had he been warned about it, was still beyond his understanding.

What rulers like the Zamorin imagined or understood or wanted did not carry any weight with the merchants on the opposite side of the globe. Three decades after da Gama's voyage, Robert Thorne, that perceptive English merchant resident in Seville, was putting this trade in perspective: "I see that the preciousness of these things is measured by the distance that is between us, and the things we have appetite unto."[1] The conquest of distance, however, was no final solution for the merchants. What good might growing appetites and soaring values do European merchants if "these things" were not to be available when a merchant ship reached her destination? Who was to keep her sponsors informed as to what European commodities might find a local market and what they might be exchanged for? Who was to see to it that a return cargo was on hand? Was this to be left to a newly arrived captain or merchant on an incoming ship? Should that ship be permitted to lie idle in port while a return cargo was being bargained for and sailors grew restive if not downright mutinous, or ill with one of the many sicknesses prevalent in such lands?

Most of these problems could be solved by having, resident in the important ports, a representative in whom the merchant-adventurers could place trust and who would have learned enough of local language and customs to bargain successfully for the return cargoes and for their lading. In short, what was needed was a resident "factor" in each port. Such an arrangement was practically as old as trade itself, undoubtedly dating back even before the time of the Phoenicians who, in the tenth century B.C., set up a colony in Carthage on the North African coast. The consequences of a similar arrangement in the Orient of the sixteenth century A.D. would be analogous—isolated outposts inviting hostile attacks, growing military power to protect trade and traders, growing empire and the escalating costs of empire—all adding up to an eventually self-destructive situation. The difference was that in the more complex world of the sixteenth century, the sequence of events was more complicated.

Events took their inexorable way as, less than twelve months after Vasco da Gama arrived back in Lisbon, another fleet of thirteen ships under Pedro Alvares de Cabral, was on its way east. This time, as a portent of things to come, 700 soldiers were carried in the fleet. Once arrived at his destination, Cabral found that the Zamorin of Calicut, having in the meantime been worked on by Arabs who saw danger in Portuguese trade rivalry, was no longer in a friendly mood. He did nothing to protect the factor Cabral left behind, so that unfortunate individual was soon murdered. Cabral persisted and, leaving another factor behind at Cochin, sailed for home on Christmas Eve 1500. Of the original thirteen ships that had sailed with Cabral, only six survived to straggle into Lisbon between the end of June and the end of July 1501.

Such losses were taken for granted and Cabral was given command of the next Portuguese fleet for the East. But da Gama expressed a desire for that command and in such matters Vasco da Gama's wishes were almost law, so he took charge of a fleet of fifteen ships which sailed in March 1502. Fully aware that he must deal with "kings" of many small Oriental states, each suspicious of the other, da Gama made a show of military strength at Calicut, then arranged formal alliances with local rulers. These rulers now feared the power of the great ships which survived the storms of a long passage and had the power to support the weight of heavy guns of a kind whose firing would have shaken local coasting vessels to pieces. It was naval power that established and held Portugal's position in the Far East—that is, until another European nation would challenge it with even greater naval power.

In 1503, Afonso de Albuquerque went to India as Portuguese military commander. He built forts at strategic spots where traders might find refuge and where soldiers might issue forth to punish attackers and press conquests. All this cut into the old trade that had routed spices through Egypt. European traders there, notably the highly mercantile Venetians, began to grow alarmed when, in 1502, they had not found enough pepper in the markets of Alexandria to lade galleys which, four years earlier, had had to leave that port without finding stowage space for all the pepper available.

For a people whose way of life depended in large part upon a successful trade in silks and spices from the Orient, it came as a rude shock that those commodities might now make a sea journey direct to Lisbon, avoiding not only the Mediterranean but the miscellaneous charges of Oriental middlemen and the further markups by Venetian traders. Something must be done to put a stop to this situation and that might best be achieved by persuading the sultan of Egypt that he, too, was threatened with financial disaster through the loss of customs duties no longer to be paid in Egypt. Thus persuaded, the sultan undertook to attack Portuguese vessels in the Red Sea but, after a few initial successes, was totally defeated in 1509 when he had to face the new viceroy, Afonso de Albuquerque. Albuquerque's success was no cause for sorrow among the Indian princes who were finding him more just to deal with than the usual Arab traders or, for that matter, the princes in neighboring principalities.

From 1509 to the end of the seventeenth century, expedition after expedition expanded Portugal's control of Far Eastern trade. Malacca, a trade emporium strategically placed on the west coast of the Malay peninsula, fell to the Portuguese in 1511. The Moluccas—the Spice Islands proper—and the nearby spice-rich Bandas soon followed. Then came the acquisition of several important citadels along the coast of cinnamon-rich Ceylon. In no case, however, was possession absolute and final. A small nation with limited manpower, Portugal had to struggle constantly to hold what she had already gained in the East. First, ambitious native rulers must be discouraged and then, late in the century, European rivals who posed a threat in ships of a quality to challenge and defeat the Portuguese at a game in which they had previously seemed the foreordained winners.

It is well to be reminded here that whatever the Portuguese had achieved in the East by way of trade and conquest was done at the behest of and for the glory and wealth of their monarch. In contrast, both Dutch and English ventures were wholly mercantile, financed by consortiums of merchants and, though not without government encouragement, strictly private ventures. Trade depended on the exchange of commodities and that, in turn, required factors on shore.

Captain Ian Splinter Stavorinus (on leave from the Dutch Navy in which he was later to become a rear admiral) piloted a Dutch East India Company ship to the Far East and reported on what he encountered there during the years 1774 to 1778. It seems not to have changed much during the more than a century and a half since the founding of the company. Being still able to reclaim his naval rank, Stavorinus could afford to report frankly on what he saw. This he did, giving a wealth of fascinating detail.

> The authority of the governor general is almost unbounded, he possesses a most arbitrary and independent power in all matters: for there are few or no members of the council, who do not stand in need of his good offices, in some instance or other, for example, in order to obtain lucrative employments for their relations or favourites; and if this be not sufficient, to make them obey the nod of the governor, he is not destitute of the means of tormenting them, in every way and under various pretenses; nay of sending them prisoners to Europe. . . . As, therefore, those who are immediately next to him in rank, depend upon, and stand in awe of him, it follows that the servants of the Company, who are in inferior stations, feel still deeper reverence, and tremble before him, as in the presence of one, from whose arbitrary will and power, their happiness or misery wholly depends: the slavish submission with which his commands are received and executed, is, in consequence, scarcely credible: for how is it possible that freeborn Hollanders, should bow themselves so low, beneath the ignominious yoke![2]

This was precisely the kind of yoke, save for the religious

overtones, against which freeborn Hollanders had rebelled nearly two centuries before when imposed by a foreign tyrant.

It became quite evident that there were dangers to be guarded against in the choice of administrators assigned to remote outposts, as well as rivals that must be dealt with there. Throughout the seventeenth century, the Dutch were moving through the East like a Juggernaut of India which trod upon anyone standing in its path. They had, of course, begun on the Portuguese, from whom they had little to learn in the way of highhandedness and to whom they could have taught something of seamanship as well as sheer grit and determination in the face of obstacles.

One by one the Dutch forced the Portuguese out of most of their "factories," as such outposts were called, in India, on Ceylon, on Sumatra and and on the shores of the Persian Gulf. Firmly entrenched on Java, they had, by 1635, reached out to establish a factory at Formosa and, six years later, at Malacca. The year 1650 saw the Dutch menacing Portuguese fleets from a Dutch settlement on the Portuguese-discovered Cape of Good Hope. Between 1651 and 1654, they seized control of the Malabar coast, except for that enduring Portuguese enclave of Goa, and forced the Portuguese entirely out of Ceylon by 1658, out of São Tomé and Macassar by 1670. Only the English then remained as a power to be reckoned with by the Dutch.

The English, too, had entered the East as traders, with no initial plans for conquest and administration. The first English East India Company (EIC) fleet sailed in 1600, but with no instructions to set up a "factory." From 1601 to 1612, EIC voyages, some pushing as far east as Japan, were "Separate Voyages," individual subscribers grouping together to share costs and reap profits which might amount to 100 percent or more on each voyage. On the third separate voyage in 1608, Captain

William Hawkins landed at Swally Roads, on the Malabar (west) coast of India near Surat, only to be told by the Portuguese established there that he could not remain to do business. Infuriated that the fate of the "Invincible Armada," which had sailed to disaster twenty years before, had taught the Portuguese no respect for British power, the English captain, nephew of the formidable Sir John Hawkins, accepted an invitation from the Grand Mogul to remain at his court. As he explained in a letter to the EIC directors in London, "so I shall do you good service, and feather my nest." Nest feathering was presently to become an earmark of the company's factors stationed in the East.

Leaving for England in 1616, Hawkins was succeeded at the Mogul court by a cleverer, more observant man, Sir Thomas Roe (1616–1619) who, though treated with respect by the Mogul, was able to achieve little more than Hawkins beyond the establishing of a British "factory" at Surat. Undazzled by the luxury he saw all about him, repelled by the violence and cruelty he occasionally had to witness, Sir Thomas kept eyes and mind open. He also kept himself free of any hint of corruption, accepting from the Grand Mogul no more than a single gift—a jewel-encrusted gold goblet in which the Mogul had offered him a drink—and shocking the Mogul by his rejection of the proffered gift of a royal concubine.

The letters of Sir Thomas that have survived the years are models of perceptiveness for any age. On 24 November 1616, he sent a letter by ship to the EIC directors in London:

> The king had peace with the *Portugueses*, and
> will never make a constant war, except first we
> displant them; then his greatness will step in
> for a share of the benefit; which dares not
> partake of the peril. . . . You can never oblige

them by any benefits, and they will sooner fear
than love you. Your residence you need not
doubt, as long as you tame the *Portugueses*,
therefore avoid all other change as unnecessary.
At my first arrival I understood a fort was very
necessary, but experience teaches me we are
refused it to our own advantage. If he would
offer me ten, I would not accept of one. . . .
The charge is greater than the trade can bear,
for to maintain a garrison will eat out the profit:
an hundred men will not keep it, for if once
the *Portugueses* see you take that course, they
will use all their endeavours to supplant you. A
war and traffick are incompatible. By my consent you shall never engage yourselves but at
sea, where you are like to gain as often as to
lose. The *Portugueses*, notwithstanding their
many rich residences, are beggared by keeping
of soldiers, and yet their garrisons are but
mean. . . . It has been also the error of the
Dutch, who seek plantations here by the sword.
. . . Let this be received as a rule, that if you
will profit, seek it at sea, and in quiet trade.
. . . One disaster would either discredit you, or
ingage you in a war of extreme danger, and
doubtful event: besides an action so subject to
chance as war, is most unfitly undertaken, and
with most hazard, when the remoteness of the
place for supplies, succours and counsel, subjects it to irrecoverable loss. . . . At sea, you
may take and leave, your designs are not publish'd."[3]

The Dutch, as Sir Thomas noted, "are arrived at
Surat from the *Red Sea* with some money and southern
commodities. I have done my best to disgrace them, but
could not turn them out without further danger. They

come on the same ground as we stand on, fear of their ships, against which I suppose you will not warrant the subjects of this king. Your comfort is, here are goods enough for both."[4]

Neither company, however, was taking much comfort then. In 1613 the Dutch made tentative approaches to the English for a treaty of coöperation in India, which having failed, there followed six years of contention during which Sir Thomas Roe had done "his best to disgrace them." In 1619 another joint attempt was made to lay the growing rivalry to rest with a formal "Treaty of Defense." At the time of its proclamation, Dutch and English fleets faced one another with flags flying and yards manned, saluting one another with their cannon. But that treaty ended as soon as the smoke of the saluting guns dissipated and the never-ending strife between the two countries went on as bitterly as ever.

Few of these encounters were quite as bitter, handled quite as cold-bloodedly, or ended as fatally as the one that took place at spice-rich Amboyna in 1623. When an EIC ship, under Captain Towerson, dropped anchor in the harbor there, Dutch authorities in their fort saw in this intrusion a barefaced attempt to undercut their spice trade. They arrested the English captain and crew of over twenty-five, tortured them to extract confessions as to their suspected intentions of seizing the Dutch fort and taking over the forbidden spice trade, then murdered them. Years passed before, under Cromwell, England and the heirs of the murdered men received financial compensation from the Dutch. Less measurable consequences for both nations would be more enduring and far-reaching.

Looking on the situation in the Spice Islands from the vantage point of a later century, Captain Stavorinus wrote:

The chief, if not the sole advantage derived to

the Company from the possession of Amboyna and its dependencies, is the collection of cloves, and the mastery of this article to the exclusion of all other nations, by which they are enabled, at pleasure, to raise or lower the price.

The company would not, however, ever have succeeded in securing to themselves the exclusive trade in spice, which is spontaneously produced in all the adjacent Molucca islands, had they not endeavoured wholly to transfer and confine the cultivation of it to Amboyna, partly by subduing the princes of those islands by force of arms and prescribing to them such conditions of peace as they found convenient . . . compelling them not to sell any of the cloves produced in their dominions to any other nations, and partly by forcing them, about the middle of the last [seventeenth] century to destroy all the clove trees which grew in their territories, for which they were to receive an equivalent in money.[5]

Not a pretty picture! But not one uniquely Dutch! In December 1669, the number of permitted clove trees was set at half a million, but what number were producing that spice in 1623 can not be known. We do know by the drastic methods taken to destroy spies and interlopers that the statistics must have been regarded as a sacred trade secret.

In any case, the English company directors were forced to recognize their exclusion from the Spice Islands and any considerable share in the trade of cloves and nutmegs. They gave no thought, however, of abandoning commerce farther to the East—China and Japan—while they made up their minds to hold their own in India, from which came considerable quantities of pepper as well as other desirable commodities. The consequences of all this were many, most of them unforeseen at the time.

"If you will profit," Sir Thomas Roe had written, "seek it at sea."[6] Fear of great foreign ships in suspicious local ports would do it. Such ships would be increasingly feared as they grew in size. Moreover, greater size could allow for larger cargoes and thus would eventually turn out to be economical. So there were developed at the company's shipyard at Deptford on the Thames the famous great East Indiamen that for two centuries were the admiration of sailors everywhere. Their size and speed offered the advantage of making them formidable both to the Malay pirates who delighted in harassing European ships and to competing European vessels—not only Dutch, Portuguese, and French, but also English rivals who were only in 1657, under Cromwell, forced to bow to the monopolistic power of the EIC.

By the then-renewed charter, the Indian trade was to be exclusively in the hands of a single joint stock company—a newer, larger company which bought up factories, forts, and concessions that had been granted to the old. It added more territory, coined money, commanded fortresses and troops, and formed alliances. In short, it had become a nation within a nation, exercising both civil and criminal jurisdiction, drawing up treaties that decided both war and peace in areas over which the Company presided. Eventually, the home government could not escape becoming involved.

By 1689, the EIC directors, shutting their eyes to what the distant future could bring, passed a resolution for the guidance of their "servants" in India. "The increase of our revenue in India is the subject of our care, as much as our trade: 'tis that must maintain our force when twenty accidents may interrupt our trade: 'tis that must make us a nation in India; without that we are but a great number of interlopers, united by his majesty's royal charter, fit only to trade where nobody of power thinks it their interest to prevent us; and upon this account it is that the wise Dutch, in all their general advices that we have seen, write ten paragraphs concerning their government for one paragraph they write concerning trade."[7]

Even had any of the company directors been reminded of the advice given by Sir Thomas Roe, they would have dismissed it as the overcautiousness of an outdated fogey: "Beware of scattering your goods and engaging your stock in various parts of the country, and engaging your stock and servants far into the country, for the time will come when all these kingdoms will be in combustion, and a few years war will not decide the inveterate malice laid up against the day of vengeance."[8]

15

Factors—Theory and Practice

Whatever decisions may have been reached in London or Amsterdam or anywhere else in Europe, whatever the size of the ships voyaging to the East, it was the individuals who went out to serve their companies who were the deciding element in the future. What were their motives? What persuaded them to risk life and limb so far from home? Did they know anything of the peoples they were undertaking to do business with? And how did these men from Europe fit themselves into alien lands with turbulent histories and trying climates? In the answers to such questions would be found the future of the trading companies whose power both in the East and at home seemed to be expanding indefinitely.

Sir Thomas Roe had seen the pitfalls as early as 1616 and had warned company directors who were as deaf as is usual with powerful men being given good advice. From Roe's letters, it soon appeared that many, if not most of the company servants had gone East only for the personal fortunes they hoped to accumulate through private dealings with native princes and nobles. Roe had not hesitated to express his disapproval of that state of affairs: "Concerning private trade, my opinion is that you should absolutely prohibit it, and execute forfeitures; for your business will be better done. All your loss is not in the goods brought home: I see here inconveniences you think not of. I know this is harsh to all men, and seems hard; men profess they come not for bare wages: but you will take away this plea if you give wages to their content; and then you know what you part from, but then you must make good choice of your servants and use fewer."[1] He might have added that except for con men (or whatever the seventeenth-century word for that type may have been) men on the make are rarely endowed with personalities to win friends among the people they are bent on exploiting.

Had the company followed Roe's advice, the history of the EIC might have been happier. However, neither the English nor the Dutch company directors seemed to succeed, even though they should have grown increasingly aware of the need, in making "good choice of servants" or being willing to part with the funds to "give wages to their content." Only the most ambitious and poor young men would have happily left home for the vaguely defined rewards actually promised them in a foreign land. The doubtful possibility of fame could hardly have tempted seventeenth-century Europeans to desert familiar ways of life for the totally unknown. Few socially and financially successful men would have been tempted to enter company service unless they were also endowed with soaring ambition to win still greater wealth and power. This would have been especially true if they had taken care to inform themselves of the risks of the journey and the problems to be dealt with by Europeans trying to settle and do business in such far and alien lands.

What most company servants who accepted underpaid positions must have already informed themselves of all too well was the possibility of lining their pockets with Eastern treasure. Many a company man went east as poor as a church mouse, to return years later as a filthy rich "nabob," often to lord it over the stay-at-homes. Occasionally a nabob managed to win immortality, as when Elihu Yale (1648–1721), living in London in luxury suitable for the Oriental potentates he had known, helped convert the struggling young Collegiate School of Connecticut into Yale University.

For another company servant, the results far out-reached the early expectations of himself and his family. Robert Clive, born in 1725, had seemed so untamably wild that his father, despairing of making anything of his son, arranged to send the lad off to India as a company clerk. Seemingly a failure at everything, including two attempts at suicide, young Clive arrived in India at the age of eighteen to become a conspicuously successful military officer by the time he was twenty-eight. The EIC clerk whose company salary had been five pounds a year (with an additional forty pounds allowed for expenses) had become by then not only a national hero but a fabulously wealthy man, thanks to the kind of "private trade" that Sir Thomas Roe had so frowned upon.

Clive's mid-eighteenth-century defeat of England's French rivals in India may have won him popular acclaim at home but it did not prevent his being forced to defend himself and his fortune before Parliament. He did this in a memorable speech that revealed some of the temptations company servants faced in the East. Reminding his critics that it had been his exertions that had led to the enrichment and increased power of the East India Company, Clive stoutly insisted that he was rather deserving of praise for the moderation which had marked his proceedings. He boasted that a great prince had been dependent upon his pleasure, an opulent city had lain at his mercy, its richest bankers had bid against each other for his smiles. Vaults piled on either hand with gold and jewels were thrown open to him. He could easily have helped himself to a greater fortune than he actually had. He won exoneration but a few years later, in 1774, a desperately ill man, he succeeded in his third attempt at suicide.

A legend in his own time, Clive's financial success sent many a young Englishman trying to follow his example in the East. Among them was Warren Hastings (1732–1818), initially as poor as Clive though descended from landed gentry dispossessed under Cromwell. Hastings wanted money to buy back the ancestral estate. By 1774, the year of Clive's death, Hastings had arrived at the governor-generalship of India. A man of diplomatic ability, he mastered local languages and thus had enabled himself to communicate effectively and form friendships with the people of India. He so consolidated English power there that by 1783, when England lost her American empire, she had, through this EIC servant, gained an empire in India. The army commander just defeated in America, Lord Cornwallis, was sent there as governor-general.

Hastings was no more than Clive able to escape accusations of corruption in office. He, too, had to defend himself before Parliament, but this time it would be a trial lasting seven long years which, though the final verdict was in his favor, left him practically penniless. He had, however, managed to buy back the ancestral estate where he lived until his death in 1818, at the age of 86, supported by an annuity granted him by the company.

The corruption so rampant in British India, as it had been also in Portuguese India, remained so in Dutch-controlled lands, too. It was less a fault of any particular governor than of those temptations constantly set before ambitious clerks. It was then too late by two centuries to act upon Sir Thomas Roe's warnings, but the Earl of

Chatham, William Pitt (1708–1778) similarly characterized the situation: "India teems with iniquities so rank
as to smell to heaven and earth." That smell of iniquity
grew strongest around the East India Compny, whose
end, already foreshadowed, was finally determined with
the Indian Mutiny of 1858. Once the mutiny was
quelled, power in India formally passed to the British
government and the centuries-old EIC, long since independent of the spice trade which had started it all, came
to an end.

The problems were by no means uniquely those of
the English. The Dutch company faced similar problems
abroad and accusations at home. VOC directors were
increasingly denounced for nepotism and corruption.
With each charter renewal, demands for reforms increased so that the company's end was already in sight
by the latter half of the eighteenth century when the
French Revolution, followed by Napoleon's invasion of
Holland, brought about the demise of the Dutch East
India Company. Dutch hegemony in Java and Sumatra,
however, continued until the onset of the Second World
War, as did the British in India.

Twenty years before the VOC came to an end,
Captain Stavorinus drew a fascinating word picture of the
way expatriate Hollanders lived in the East—not funda-
mentally different from the life-styles of other displaced
Europeans. Batavia, Stavorinus wrote, "is situated very
near the sea, in a fertile plain." He follows this with a
description of the city's layout and of the governing
hierarchy. Of the citizens themselves, he recorded:
"Europeans, whether Dutch, or of any other nation, and
in whatever station they are, live at Batavia in nearly the
same manner,"[2] rising at daybreak, as is customary in
tropic lands, spending some time sitting half-dressed in
their doorways, breakfasting on coffee or tea, finally
dressing themselves in a stiffly correct manner more

suitable to cool Holland than to their steaming tropical environment.

As for social activity, "convivial gaiety seems to reign among them, and yet it is linked with a kind of suspicious reserve, which pervades all stations, and all companies, and is the consequence of arbitrary and jealous government. The least word, that may be wrested to an evil meaning, may bring on very serious consequences, if it reach the ears of the person who is aggrieved, whether in fact or in imagination. I have heard people assert, that they would not confide in their own brothers, in this country."[3]

All this falsely "convivial gaiety" was a perquisite of the men only. Women, whether Dutch-born or native-born wives or Javanese concubines, were of barely secondary importance, their social needs and intellectual potential totally ignored. With no social activities to distract them, nothing interesting to do, women were left free to concentrate their undirected energies on bitter rivalries of unimaginable pettiness. Children were left to the care of Javanese nursemaids.

There was no distinction between the sexes in the damaging effects on health of living in Batavia, where the "most disagreeable circumstance attending residence" was "the great degree of mortality which prevails there, especially among transient visitors, or people that first arrive"—long-time residents that survived having acquired some degree of resistance to those dread tropical diseases. "The English who circumnavigated the globe (1768–1770) and had experienced almost every vicissitude of climate, declared that *Batavia* was not only the most unhealthy place they had seen, but that this circumstance was sufficient defense or preservative against any hostile attempt, as the troops of no nation would be able to withstand, nor would any people in their senses, without absolute necessity, venture to encounter this pestilential atmosphere."[4]

Absolute necessity had faced that particular circum-navigating vessel, the *Endeavour* under the famous Cap-tain James Cook, when a keel-scraping accident off the Australian coast had forced it to visit Batavia for repairs by the expert shipwrights of neighboring Onrust Island. Naturalist of the *Endeavour* was Sir Joseph Banks, who kept a journal of the voyage. When the ship dropped anchor off Batavia on 9 October 1770, a boat with officer and crew hurried out to enquire whence the new arrival came and what might be her business.

"Both himself and his people," Banks wrote of the men in the boat, "were almost as Spectres, no good omen of the healthyness of the country we were arrived at; our people however who might truly be calld rosy and plump, for we had not a sick man among us, jeered and flouted much at their brother sea mans white faces."[5] They were no longer jeering by Christmas day when their repaired ship was putting to sea, "There was not I believe a man in the ship but who gave his utmost in getting up the anchor, so compleatly tird was every one of the unwholesome air of this place. We had buried eight people."[6] They were to bury yet more as, on the return voyage, dysentery added its blows to already weakened systems.

The Dutch Captain Stavorinus was even more ex-plicit as to the unattractive aspects of the place: "A dismal succession of stinking mudbanks, filthy bogs, and stagnant pools announce to more senses than one the poisonous nature of this dreadful climate."[7] Time was to suggest that it was less the climate than those stagnant pools and stinking mudbanks that were responsible for the unhealthiness of a place which, when founded in 1619, had seemed to hold much promise. The harbor was still outstanding, but eighty years after Batavia's founding, an earthquake more terrible than those its inhabitants had grown used to, sent down upon the city's environs mudslides that choked flowing rivers and turned them into stagnating pools where mosquitoes bred in great numbers. Banks casually mentioned the mosquito nuisance but was totally unaware that such tiny insects could have anything to do with the fevers which so harassed everyone in Batavia. It would be over a century before anyone came to acknowledge those as vectors of diseases, notably of that fever and ague which we now call "malaria."

In the eighteenth century, long before any organism responsible for a human disease had been recognized, only a madman would have presumed to blame a mosquito for carrying malarial fever from victim to victim. Yet the grimly acknowledged fact was that about half the Dutch East India Company's employees stationed in Batavia died each year, their condition worsened by the frequent bloodlettings which physicians saw then as a sovereign treatment for practically everything. Life expectancy was a bit better in the Javanese outposts but that still only meant a mortality far higher than anyone of our times could accept with resignation. Small wonder that the VOC employees distracted themselves with falsely convivial gatherings such as Captain Stavorinus described. It was also understandable that the accumulation of fortunes to be enjoyed (later, with luck) in the less lethal climate of their homelands became the motivating force behind so many actions of the companies and their employees.

The routes to wealth and leisure were various. Military glory could only be for specially gifted men. Influence, if a man had it to sell, could prove a profitable commodity but its value depended upon encountering the right purchaser at the right time. Trade remained the chosen route even after that old standby, spices, began to be less profitable than it once had been. Jaded European palates and the soaring prices demanded by monopolists combined forces to limit the incomes spices could bring in. By the late eighteenth century, even the trading companies were seeing the handwriting on the wall, at least as far as the spice trade was concerned.

Even with inadequate salaries, administrative expenses continued to soar. Ships had to be built, equipped, supplied with ammunition as well as basic foodstuffs. A ship strong enough to survive as many as six round trips was a rarity. Representatives had to continue to dispose of trade goods sent out to bring in the money to pay for return cargoes. As Captain Stavorinus viewed it, administrative expenses "must be defrayed out of the profits of the cloves, nutmeg, and mace . . . but can any favourable expectations of future advantage be entertained on this head, when we consider the great decrease which is experienced in the sale of the first named spice. Three million pounds remaining in the warehouses at Batavia, of which no more than one fifteenth part can be annually disposed of in the Indies, together with the stock on hand in Holland, large enough to supply the consumption of Europe for a space of ten years, and the quantities of cloves that from time to time are committed to the flames by the Company, in order to lessen their superabundant stock, form proofs enough of the decrease of the clove trade."[8] It sounds very much as if the over-competent Dutch were killing their "golden goose."

It began to look as if the Far Eastern companies and their employees must either face bankruptcy or find new sources of income. This meant finding some uniquely Eastern product or products for which demand could be both created and supported in Europe and possibly increased in the Orient itself. Again it would be plant products, tea from China toward which early English voyages had tended being an important one destined to play an unanticipated role in international affairs.

Already in 1596, young Jan Huyghen van Linschoten, visiting Japan as clerk of the travelling Archbishop of Goa, was reporting on "a certaine drinke, which is a pot of hot water" wherein was steeped, "the powder of a certaine herbe called *Cha*" impressively served in highly valued porcelain cups. By the 1630s, this tea habit had reached Europe where the viewers-with-alarm to be expected at all times with strange new products, began whispering that it was an oriental habit of great danger to human health. Undaunted, the Dutch took to the habit both in Batavia and back home in Holland, then began a public relations campaign to popularize it.

By the 1660s tea had arrived at a point corresponding to that where spices had been two centuries before. Twenty-three pounds of tea, valued at fifty shillings a pound, was then considered a princely gift, quite acceptable to King Charles II of England. Perhaps that monarch had acquired the tea habit from his queen, the Portuguese Catherine of Braganza, who, in 1662, brought it to England along with a naval base at Bombay, as part of her dowry. The poet Edmund Waller, ever responsive to the political and social fashions of his day, exalted both the queen and her favorite beverage:

> Venus her myrtle, Phoebus hath his bays;
> Tea both excels, which she vouchsafes to
>   praise.
> The best of queens and best of herbs we owe
> To that bold nation which the way did show
> To the far regions where the sun doth rise,
> Whose rich productions we so richly prize,
> The Muse's friend, tea doth our fancy aid,
> Repress those vapours which the head invade,
> And keeps the palace of the soul serene,
> Fit on her birthday to salute the Queen.

Ordinary Englishmen took happily to the royally sponsored habit, gathering over cups of tea to discuss issues of the day. Charles II, uncomfortably recalling his father's fate, began to see in such gatherings the makings of a subversive attitude towards royal power. The rebellion was to come, but not in his time nor in a way that he could possibly have envisaged.

With the tea habit growing profitable, some Englishman saw in that Chinese shrub a worthwhile crop for Far Eastern lands other than China. Somewhere, in or near the highlands of India which they now controlled, there should be areas whose climate and soil conditions sufficiently approximated those of China for tea to prove a profitable crop there. With this in mind, they sent out collectors of seed who were to observe, in particular, the planting, harvesting, and curing of tea in its native habitat. Thus, they hit upon Assam, next door to Burma, as a suitable place to start a tea-growing business which, if properly managed, might come to supplement, if not supplant, the once thriving trade in that Indian spice, pepper.

Ironically, though tea could be successfully grown in Assam, the East India Company showed little enthusiasm for transferring their tea business from China to India. Chinese tea had become an important point in the three-cornered trade which EIC directors saw as vital to produce funds needed to support their "factories" in India—Chinese tea to Britain, British manufactured goods to India and, to complete the triangle, India-produced opium to China. It was a fateful decision.

By the 1770s, the East India Company was so near bankruptcy that the stay-at-home Englishmen whose funds were invested in the company began to grow alarmed. Something must be done to save the company and their funds! It was then that Lord North had his bright idea—place a tax on tea, not a very large one, but yet enough so that the tea-drinking American colonials should help raise the money needed to salvage the shaky Far Eastern company. What that "taxation without representation" actually raised, as every American school-child knows, was howls of fury, to be followed by the

Boston Tea Party and the American War of Independence. So subversive had tea turned out to be!

The notorious three-cornered trade would turn out to be equally disastrous in another way. Initially opium was looked upon as just one more crop, accepted by growers and shippers as a legitimate article of international trade. What a drug did to its purchasers was just not the shippers' business except that it should produce profit for middlemen as well as for those possessing opium-producing poppy fields in India. Captain Stavorinus reported he had been told that the opium harvest there amounted annually to "upwards of a million pounds"—worth a great deal but not unless it could be assured of purchasers. Finding purchasers and keeping them satisfied was the problem.

Enlarging trade also meant enlarging the consuming public. That could best be done by encouraging opium-smoking among the Chinese. As early as 1796, however, the Chinese government had grown alarmed and tried to limit opium use by forbidding importation of the drug. So little was this interdiction heeded that within forty years the importation of opium into China had increased tenfold. Clipper ship masters, English and American, made fortunes in the business, as did corrupt Chinese customs officials. By 1838, alarmed at the devastating effect this flood of opium was having, the Chinese emperor tried to enforce the old edicts, only to find himself, in 1840, in an "opium war" with Britain. The rising young English politician William Gladstone characterized this conflict as: "A war more unjust in its origins, a war more calculated to cover this country with permanent disgrace, I do not know and have not read of. The British flag is hoisted to protect an infamous contraband traffic; and if it never was hoisted but as it is now hoisted on the coast of China, we should all recoil in horror."[9]

Gladstone's biographer, Lord Morley, went into

more detail: "There was no pretense that China was in the wrong, for, in fact, the British Government had sent out orders that opium smugglers should not be shielded, but the orders arrived too late, and war having broken out, Great Britain felt compelled to see it through."[10] A pretty feeble excuse for a disgraceful war! But Britain triumphed and by the 1842 Treaty of Nanking, the Chinese were forced to pay an indemnity of 600,000 pounds for the opium they had confiscated and destroyed. Four treaty ports, plus Hong Kong, were also part of Britain's booty. Hong Kong presently became an important base for smuggling into China the opium which, strangely, was not even mentioned in the treaty.

As smuggling increased, Chinese opposition to opium importation increased. This resulted in another, even more disastrous opium war (1856–1858) after which opium continued to gain entry into China "at less duty than the English levied on Chinese silks." In 1871, a distinguished witness before the House of Commons stated baldly that England had forced the Chinese government to allow their subjects to take opium—something many Britons were long to find highly embarrassing. Fifty years later, an increasingly shamefaced Britain agreed to a gradual reduction in opium importation into China until the amount was reduced to zero. It was by an agreement that China fulfilled to the letter, thus freeing herself from the curse of opium.

Long before that date, both the Dutch and English East India Companies had come to an end. The Dutch had a hand in the opium trade which they found very profitable largely in the lands over which they had control. As Captain Stavorinus recorded: "Opium is a very important production, both for the inland trade and that which is carried on by sea, to the coast of Coromandel and Batavia . . . all that is exported, comes down the *Ganges*, through *Bengal*. More than one hundred thousand pounds weight of this drug is annually shipped by our Company's vessels, and is consumed at *Java*, the *Moluccas*, and other places in the eastern part of *Asia*. The natives of all those countries are very fond of it, smoking it together with their tobacco, or chewing it unmixed."

Known and used almost from the dawn of history, opium, produced in the seed pods of a very beautiful poppy, *Papaver somniferum* (sleep-bringing poppy) was too easily salable a commodity for Europeans trading in the East to disparage. It would never have occurred to most people, as it might in our own times, to think themselves to blame for encouraging a disastrous habit. The Britons who stood up in Parliament to accuse their own nation were the exception rather than the rule. As long as they remained, trading companies remained dedicated to their original purpose—trade, whatever the consequences.

Captain Stavorinus felt no need to apologize for Dutch participation in the opium trade, explaining how the Dutch handled it through a society that was not an official part of the VOC.

> A society was established at Batavia during the government of Baron van Imhof, for the opium trade, which is still in existence. . . . Every chest of opium stands the company in two hundred and fifty, and sometimes three hundred rixdollars, and is delivered to the society for five hundred, and sometimes more. On the other hand the Company is bound to sell this drug to no other. The retail of it produces large profits, as the society make eight or nine hundred rixdollars, and more, of every chest of about 133 pounds. The gain would be more considerable if the monopoly could be strictly enforced, for the whole quantity of opium consumed in the eastern parts of India . . . but

those who engage in this illicit trade, take too many precautions, to run any danger of detection. The smuggling trade which the English carry on, in this article, in the eastern islands, and by way of *Malacca*, is also extremely detrimental to the society.[11]

Detriment to consumers' health seems to have carried no weight at all to an eighteenth-century Dutch or English company whose avowed reason for existence was trade. Yet for both companies, the end was in sight, control of their world empires passing presently to home governments until World War II. By then, spice crops of the Far East had receded into the background and other tropical crop plants—rubber and quinine, for instance—had soared in importance. Expeditions of a kind which had once aimed at locating lands still exploitable by European adventurers had turned into expeditions for locating new plants or new varieties of old plants that could be grown on plantations of familiar lands. Inevitably, agricultural experts displaced trading factors.

16

Peter Pepper Has the Last Word

It was not to have been expected that merchants of other European nations would always look on resignedly while the Dutch and English raked in fortunes which the Portuguese and Spanish had once claimed as uniquely theirs. In several nations, trading companies arose, survived briefly, then went the way of those nations which had started it all. The only one that showed any promise of permanence was the French company which was also the only important one not to admit its chief inspiration to have been spices. Nevertheless, it would be the French—or, at least, a Frenchman—that would have the last word on spice monopolies anywhere.

Jean Baptiste Colbert, the gifted Minister of Finance for Louis XIV, was the man who, in 1663, was responsible for the founding of the French East India Company. Its headquarters at Madagascar could conveniently serve as a way station for regular trade with India and Persia. Unlike the English and Dutch companies, but like the Portuguese undertakings in the East, this was no merchant-organized and controlled company. The state—that is, Louis XIV, as he explicitly claimed—had to find the money for backing the company either out of his own treasury or the pockets of reluctant donors.

In 1673, a grant by the local Indian ruler, who may have thought competition healthy, allowed the French to establish a factor at Pondichery, about ninety miles south of Madras on the Coromandel (east) coast. This would long remain headquarters for the French on Indian soil, being supplemented in 1742 with other "factories," one at Chandernagore in Bengal and another at Mahe on the Malabar coast north of Calicut. In that same year, with Joseph Francois Dupleix becoming governor of Pondichery, the French occupied the small but strategically placed Mascarene Islands (later referred to as Bourbon and Ile de France, and more recently Mauritius and Reunion) to the east of Madagascar and astride the route from the Cape of Good Hope to Cape Cormorin at the southernmost tip of India. Two years later, the incessant wars with and between local rulers were exacerbated when the War of the Austrian Succession which, having broken out in Europe, set the English and French at odds in all areas of the globe. It was in the course of these struggles that Clive won his famous victory over Dupleix at Plassey and thereby established English predominance on the Indian subcontinent.

Ironically, it was not an English military genius but an imaginative and resourceful young Frenchman who prepared the final blow for the great spice trade that had enmeshed diverse Europeans for so long. The idea behind it was not totally new with him, as witness a 1661 document in the British Museum entitled, "A proposall for Removing of Spices and Other Plants from the East to the West Indies." Here they would be so much more conveniently grown for European use that one has to wonder why someone had not come up with such a proposal long before.

Other Englishmen, possibly persuaded by the un-identified author of that proposal, were thinking in the same direction. John Evelyn, the famous diarist who also served as a member of the Council of Foreign Planta-tions, noted for February 12, 1672, that at a council meeting, "we entered on inquiries on improving the plantations by silks, galls, flax, senna, etc. and consid-ered how nutmegs and cinnamon might be obtained and brought to Jamaica."[1] This seems to have been an idea before its time for Evelyn makes no further mention of possible Jamaican spice plantations as he would have done had enough council members been truly interested in the proposition.

Jamaica could have been the right place for such a venture since the soil was fertile, the climate right, and the latitude, which determines the crucial relationship between hours of daylight and darkness, also right. What was needed further was a man with a way of thinking unconventional enough to reject the belief that spice trees and the Orient were inseparable—a point of view hallowed by centuries of acceptance. Company servants, of whatever nationality, were unlikely to challenge a belief upon which company fortunes had been founded even though it must have been gradually becoming obvious that spices were a commodity doomed to yield in importance to other products.

Interestingly, the possibility of transplanting spice trees from their original habitat was never rejected by the Spice Islanders themselves. Transplanting young trees from the wild, or just gathering, planting, and tending seeds and their shoots, was what had started their own plantations in spots more accessible to them than those where wild plants originally took root.

Limiting spice crops by limiting the numbers of trees permitted to grow is implicit in Captain Stavorinus's statement that, however hard the Dutch East India Company might try to limit spice-growing areas, the effort was doomed to failure because "there are too many islands, and too widely dispersed, that produce these commodities, of which neither they not their allies are in possession." Actually, some of the smaller spice-growing islands seemed to be in the possession of no one.

S. H. Wilcocke, who in 1798 prepared a translation of Stavorinus's book, adding copious notes, wrote: "A short time before the coming of the Portuguese to Amboyna, the Cerammers of Cambello secretly brought some mother cloves in hollow bamboos from Machian, whence they were propagated all over Ceram, Amboyna, and the neighboring islands, and in the space of fifty or sixty years the whole of Hoewamoebil [a peninsula jutting out from Ceram] was covered with them. This was told the Dutch when first they came to Cambello, some of the trees first planted were shown to them . . . the memory of it is likewise preserved in the traditionary songs of the Amboynese."[2]

Anyone who listened to and understood such songs would have realized that the idea of transplanting spice trees among the Spice Islands was a viable one. If there, why not elsewhere as long as environmental conditions were right? It was a thought which the Dutch were not likely to encourage.

Without encouragement, and undoubtedly with appropriate secrecy, the French East India Company had, as early as 1729, drawn up plans for sending a vessel to one or more of the many small uninhabited Spice Islands to steal young spice trees for transplanting in French-controlled soil. That particular plan came to nothing, perhaps for lack of real enthusiasm, perhaps for lack of a suitable person to carry it out. What was needed was a man like the flamboyant young Frenchman, appropriately named Pierre Poivre (Peter Pepper), endowed with a lively curiosity about the remote places of the world and a gift for the mastery of strange new languages.

Born in 1719, Poivre enrolled himself at the age of twenty among the missionaries of St. Joseph and was soon happily on his way to mission stations in distant Cochin China (later Indochina and then Vietnam). The young missionary was soon neglecting his devotions for the study of local languages, as well as of the exotic peoples and customs. He soon involved himself in some sort of scrape which so angered his missionary superiors that they put him on a French ship bound for home.

The War of the Austrian Succession with both the French and the English involved had then just broken out in Europe. The French ship on which young Poivre was travelling was attacked by an English ship, an encounter in which the young Frenchman suffered a serious wound in his arm. The English held him briefly as a prisoner, then released him to the custody of the Dutch at Batavia, where he promptly set to work learning all he could about clove and nutmeg plantations. By the time he could again head for home, his mind was full of plans for growing spices in colonies controlled by France.

The voyage home, after detouring to French outposts at Madras and Pondichery, took him to Madagascar via the French-controlled Mascarenes, where he studied soil and climate conditions and reported of Madagascar that there could be no doubt that if the French India Company, which was in possession of the trade of this island, gave proper encouragement to agriculture, it would in a short time make rapid progress. The islands of Bourbon and France would find here certain resources while the French squadrons bound for India, who put into the Isle of France for refreshments, would always find abundance of provisions brought from Madagascar. Thus they would not be subjected to the necessity of losing their time at the cape, or at Batavia, while the enemies of France conquered their settlements and devastated their trade. From supplying ships with fresh vegetables, fruits, and meats, to producing cargoes of spices was not, in young Poivre's mind, too long a jump.

Reaching France after a second brief episode as a prisoner of the English, Poivre contacted the directors of the French Company of the Indies to urge upon them two projects he thought important. One was the building up of direct commercial relations with Indochina, where as yet no other European country had seized a dominant position. The other was the securing and transplanting of spice-producing trees to the Mascarenes, notably to the Isle of France. So convincing were his arguments that he presently, as an appointed representative of the French monarch, returned to Indochina. He soon succeeded in arranging the first of his projects.

Transplanting spices was bound to be a more complicated matter since the natives of lands where spices grew had long since been made to understand how much men from afar valued their trees. They, as well as the trading company settled there, had a stake in maintaining their spice monopoly. The Dutch, with their tremendous financial investment threatened, had even more urgent reasons for taking no chances that other nations should succeed in securing the means to grow spices. For this reason, they had forbidden strangers to set foot on islands where there were spice plantations. They extirpated trees that grew outside the confines of their plantations. Then, to make doubly sure, they saw to it that spices sent to other lands had been so treated that they could not sprout. Nutmegs they treated with lime, which also served as a preservative. Treatment with steam or boiling water was another way of preventing viability—as, halfway around the world, Brazilian Indians similarly undertook to deprive rubber seeds of their power to propagate or as the Aymaras of the Peruvian Altiplano tried to do with quinine. It was all in vain for the genius of plants is that a small handful of viable seeds can nullify such efforts.

Eventually Java was to have rubber and quinine plantations, just as the Isle of France and other French colonies were to have spice trees. Undoubtedly these owed their start to one or another of the uninhabited Moluccas where Pierre Poivre managed, during the 1750s, to secure nineteen clove seedlings to carry with him to the Isle of France. By the time his voyage ended, only twelve of those seedlings were still alive and, of these, only five survived to take root and grow in Mascarene soil. Five seedlings were enough to grow into great trees capable of producing a multitude of seeds.

In France, however, the company's directors seemed to be losing interest in giving support to young Poivre's grand scheme. Discouraged, he left his surviving seedlings on the Isle of France to the tender mercies of a gardener and retired, in 1757, to his estate near Lyons. Not a man given to inaction nor to accept happily the rejection of an important scheme, he worked to re-awaken interest among French authorities and, possibly through pressure judiciously applied by scientifically-minded friends, finally succeeded. By 1766, Poivre was being offered the governorship of the Isle of France, where he would now have the authority he had previously lacked and the means of underwriting spice plantations.

He could now send out expeditions to gather spice seeds from right under Dutch noses. One such expedition went in 1769 to 1770, a second in 1771 to 1772. By the time the second one returned, Poivre had established his private botanical garden, Mon Plaisir, where he could follow his botanical bent as he might choose. By 1772, Mon Plaisir could boast 400 kidnapped nutmeg plants, 10,000 viable nutmegs to plant, seventy clove seedlings and a box full of mother-cloves, some already sprouting. With both soil and climate, as well as latitude, suitable for clove trees, Poivre's garden presently included an orchard of 8,000 clove seedlings and some nutmegs.

Plant introduction generally seems to have been Governor Poivre's hobby, for before he left the island for good in 1773, he had started a great variety of plants new to the Isle of France: breadfruit; mangoes; mangosteens; tea plants; camphor trees; date and sago palms; and, of course, cinnamon trees. He also tried apples, pears, and peaches but whether these primarily temperate fruits throve on that tropical isle, he was not to know before his departure.

Once more settled near Lyons, Poivre maintained his interest in the plantings he had left behind, corresponding with enthusiasm with a former neighbor, Jean Nicolas Céré, who undertook to care for the plantings at Mon Plaisir. Céré further sent spice seedlings to planters on the other Mascarene, Isle Bourbon, trying to encourage them by correspondence.

In all this, Céré seems to have received no more official encouragement than had Poivre. Poivre's own written pleas to Governor Dumesle on behalf of the plants only seemed to arouse antagonism. A thoroughly exasperated governor finally gave vent to his feelings in an angry letter: "For you, M. le Poivre, the first and foremost care as Intendant of the Ile de France seems to have been to look after your precious spice trees. I have wider and more important things to consider. It is evidently not enough for you to have spoken to me about cloves and nutmegs for days, but now you continue to harp on the same subject. Let me tell you frankly, I am sick of the very word 'spice tree.' "[3] So low had spices fallen in the estimation of men and nations!

Not a man to accept such a judgment as final, Poivre kept on trying to indoctrinate important people in France. Céré wrote to let him know that some of the trees he had transplanted had flowered and appeared about to bear fruit. In a few years, these would be producing sufficiently profitable crops to be sold in Asia where spices were more in demand than in Europe.

It was the politics of the situation that finally convinced the stay-at-homes. Once the Dutch realized that their spice monopoly had been permanently broken, they were far more amenable to a commercial treaty with France. But this could not come to pass unless the planting and raising of spice trees on the Mascarenes was given priority status in France. Those trees on the Isle of France must be put under the care of a man prepared to dedicate himself to the undertaking.

All these arguments attained their goal in March 1775, when Céré received an official appointment as director of the "Jardin du Roi," as Mon Plaisir became after the king sanctioned the government purchase of Poivre's estate on the Isle of France. A convenient summer residence for the island's governors, the garden was destined to win special fame among the world's botanists.

From his appointment on, all thoughts and efforts of the garden's director were devoted to improving spice cultivation in the Mascarenes. Clove trees throve, though at first producing smaller fruit than had been hoped. However, by the time the second generation of cloves, grown from seed produced on the islands, came into bearing, the fruit size was larger. All sizes were highly salable to Asian consumers.

Nutmegs, however, were doing less well. Few trees had survived and few survivors produced fruit. Why, was long the question—as the Dutch had intended it to be for anyone trying to break their nutmeg monopoly. It was, it turned out, due to a basic fact of life, which had rarely needed to be recognized in the wild where enough trees grew for the statistics to be in favor of fertility. Where there are few trees and those isolated from others of their kind, however, the sex life of nutmegs can loom very important.

Nutmeg trees share with a limited number of other kinds of plants the interesting quality of being sex-conscious—of belonging to one sex or the other—or, as botanists call it, dioecious. They are either male or female, not, as is more usual with plants, bearing sex organs of both kinds on a single plant. For the fertilization which must come before the formation of fruit, pollen must somehow be transferred from a male flower to the stamens of a female. This is no unique attribute of nutmegs but is shared by diverse kinds, such as date palms, and in more temperate climes, sumac. In such plants, no isolated individual, no matter how healthy, can produce seed. No female can bear fruit unless it grows close enough to a male plant for wind or insects to carry the pollen to its sex organs. Yet such plants, whatever their sex may be, give no visible signs of their sex preferences.

Thus, until a nutmeg tree has grown to maturity, no one unaware of the situation suspects why no nutmegs are produced. M. Céré's letters to fellow planters on Bourbon, even after he came to recognize the basic problem, are filled with the frustrations caused by dealing with such sex-conscious plants. He had sent an indubitably female plant, secured by layering a tree he had witnessed to be fruit-bearing, to M. le Comte de Souillac who had requested one. The slave to whose care the little plant had been entrusted, was given strict orders to throw it overboard should an English vessel capture the French one carrying him to the Ile de Bourbon. Though he must have suspected that the lone female could not by itself produce fruit, he took no chances of having a female tree fall into enemy hands.

By way of reply, the count acknowledged the arrival of the little tree, then reported a dispute between himself and a neighbor as to whose male plant should be allowed to fertilize the precious female flowers. A couple of months later, the count asked that a male plant be sent him. His female was in flower but there was no male growing at the right distance and in the right stage of pollination to asssure that the female would be properly served. In the end, a brilliant solution to the problem of sex-conscious plants was arranged—grafting male shoots onto female trees.

As if sex had not produced enough problems, internal French politics were further complicating the raising of spices on the Mascarenes. In his wisdom, the French Minister of Marine decided that the part of the French dominions where spices should grow was the French West Indies or French Guiana, possibly because he saw those regions as accessible to continued French control. He issued orders that plants be sent there from the Jardin du Roi on the Isle of France and that further spice culture there was to be discouraged, if not totally interdicted. It looks suspiciously as if Governor Maillart-Dumesle, who had previously expressed himself so spitefully on the subject of spice culture, had a hand in this decision. Having previously held a government post in Cayenne, he perhaps wished to favor that place with a crop every gardener insisted was profitable, while at the same time ridding himself of a great nuisance.

On the Mascarenes the planters who had not been consulted in the matter were embittered. Was the reward of all their efforts to accrue to the remote French West Indies? They argued and worked against the measure in vain. Though the Mascarenes would continue to act as way stations for the transfer of spice trees from the Far East, they would lose their monopoly as the Portuguese, then the Dutch, had lost theirs. In the end, anyone trying to secure a monopoly of any kind of plant was bound to lose.

It would be the same with cloves. The translator of Captain Stavorinus's book into English pointed out in his notes that "The clove-tree has, however, been successfully introduced into the West India Islands, and though the quantities hitherto brought from them, have been very insignificant, yet their constant increase suffices to show, that the culture is in an improving state; in 1797, 350 pounds were imported to London from Martinico [French owned Martinique] and in the present year (1798) 20 pounds from that island and 2981 from St. Kitts."[4]

The editor gives no hint as to how spice culture got started on English St. Kitts, but the date together with the known fact that a clove tree begins to bear fruit when about nine years old suggest that those trees on St. Kitts may have been second-generation West Indian trees, possibly bought (or stolen) from a French plantation in Cayenne or one of the French West Indian islands. By 1818, of the 78,000 pounds of cloves sold in England for that year, 70,000 pounds were said to have arrived from Cayenne, where a third or fourth generation of clove trees could have come into bearing. With such trees possiblly surviving to the ripe old age of eighty-five, any Spice Island spice monopoly would remain a thing of the past.

No such famous effort was made to transplant pepper trees to the New World, where those tiny black balls would have been looked upon by native Americans more as a source of income than as a flavoring for their food. There was a New World "pepper," of a quite distinct plant genus, which could hold its own against the Oriental *Piper nigrum*. New World Indians had always had their *Capsicum*, described by Nicholas de Monardes in his "Joyfull Newes Out of the Newe Founde Worlde," published in 1574 and, in translation, in 1577: "Also they doe bring . . . a certaine kinde of Peper, which they call long Peper, which hath a sharper taste, than the Peper which is brought from the Orientall Indias, and it doth bite more than it, and it is of a more sweete taste and of better smell, than that of Asia, or the Peper of the East India, it is a gentle spice for to dresse meates withall, and for this effect all the people in that countrie doe use it. . . . I have tasted it and it biteth more than the black Peper doeth, and it hath a more sweete taste than it. I have caused it to bee put in to dresse meates, in place of the Orientall Peper, and it giveth a gentle taste unto that as is drest therewith."[5]

Belonging to a large, strictly New World, plant genus, *Capsicum*, such peppers grow on small shrubby plants or on vines and may appear, according to species or variety, in many sizes, shapes, colors, and tastes. *Capsicum tetragonum* is particularly notable in that long ago it was introduced into Hungary, there to win favor and be cultivated on a large scale and to emerge finally as "Hungarian" paprika. In addition to giving that gentle taste to meats, *Capsicum* can supply what those dry black balls from the Orient cannot—valuable vitamins. However, none of them ever did supply the spice to history furnished by any spice native to the Far East.

A spice expert assures us that most of the spices once exclusive products of the East now grow on Caribbean islands or nearby continental America, Grenada's nutmeg being a case in point. No one now pretends to a monopoly in growing any kind of spice nor a monopoly in marketing them, as witnessed by the great variety of little cans and bottles now to be found on the spice shelves of our markets. The incredibly grim rivalries, for which so many lives and fortunes were sacrificed, are now long since laid to rest.

Notes

1 Lure and Legend
(1) I Kings 10:2
(2) Revelation 18:11, 13
(3) Motley, *History of the United Netherlands*, vol. IV, p. 245.
(4) Gibbon, *Decline and fall*, p. 1268.
(5) Polo, *Travels*, p. 96.
(6) Skrine, *Chinese central Asia*, p. 111.
(7) Letts, *Mandeville's travels*, p. 501.
(8) Polo, p. 363.
(9) Komroff, *Contemporaries of Marco Polo*, pp. 308, 309.

2 Priest Potentate John
(1) Alvares, *Prester John*, p. 99.
(2) Gibbon, p. 1272.
(3) Pliny, *Natural history*, XLII.
(4) Hakluyt, *Principall navigations*, p. 191.
(5) Ibid.
(6) Howe, *In quest of spices*, p. 61.
(7) Ibid.
(8) Ibid.

3 Prince-Navigator and Neophytes
(1) Herodotus, p. 245.

(2) Azurara, *Discovery and conquest of Guinea*, pp. 27–28.

(3) Ibid., p. 28.

(4) Ibid.

(5) Ibid., p. 31.

(6) Ibid.

4 The World Divided

(1) Morison, *Journals of Christopher Columbus*, p. 22.

(2) Hakluyt, p. 508.

(3) Ibid., p. 519.

5 Passage to India

(1) da Gama, *The three voyages*, p. xxii.

(2) Ibid., p. 52.

(3) Ibid., p. 56.

(4) Ibid., pp. 113, 114.

(5) Ibid.

(6) Ibid., p. 380.

6 To Goa—and Back?

(1) Pyrard, *The voyage of Pyrard de Laval*, pp. 180, 181, 182–84.

(2) Ibid., p. 185.

(3) Ibid., pp. 191–92.

(4) Ibid., p. 196.

(5) Ibid., p. 199.

(6) Ibid., pp. 282–83.

(7) Ibid., pp. 189–92.

(8) Ibid., p. 189.

(9) Boxer, *Tragic history*, p. 55.

(10) Ibid., p. 57.

(11) Linschoten, *The voyage to the East Indies*, p. 217.

(12) Ibid., pp. 220–21.

(13) Gama, p. 11.

7 So Noble a Captain

(1) Las Casas, *Historia de las Indias*, pp. 174, 175.

(2) Ibid.

(3) Pigafetta, *The first voyage around the world*, pp. xlii, xliv.

(4) Ibid.

(5) Ibid., p. 37.
(6) Ibid.
(7) Ibid., p. 65.
(8) Ibid., p. 102.
(9) Ibid.

8   The World Encircled
    (1) Pigafetta, p. 124.
    (2) Ibid., p. 129.
    (3) Ibid., p. 134, 135.
    (4) Ibid.
    (5) Morison, *The southern voyage*, pp. 471–72.
    (6) Ibid.

9   Route of the Manila Galleons
    (1) Prescott, *History of the conquest of Mexico*, vol. III,
        pp. 419–23.
    (2) Mitchell, *Friar Andres de Urdaneta*, p. 28.
    (3) *Colección de documentos inéditos*, pp. 98–100.
    (4) Ibid., pp. 106–9.
    (5) Mitchell, p. 137.
    (6) Ibid.
    (7) Hakluyt, pp. 550, 551.
    (8) Morga, *Sucesos de las Islas Filipinas*, p. 305.
    (9) Ibid., p. 307.
    (10) Fletcher, *The world encompassed*, p. 61.
    (11) Hakluyt, p. 512.

10 French Challengers
    (1) Howe, p. 174.
    (2) Ibid., p. 184.
    (3) Pyrard, p. 1.
    (4) Ibid., p. 5.
    (5) Ibid., p. 11, 12.
    (6) Ibid., pp. 355, 356.
    (7) Ibid.

11 The Shortest Way
    (1) Hakluyt, p. 517.
    (2) Ibid., pp. 250–58.
    (3) Ibid., p. 517.
    (4) Ibid.

(5) Ibid., p. 285.

(6) Ibid., pp. 280–92.

(7) Ibid., p. 365.

(8) Morison, *The northern voyages*, p. 605.

(9) Veer, *The three voyages of William Barents*, p. 7.

(10) Ibid., p. 37.

(11) Ibid., pp. 79–81.

(12) Ibid., p. 306.

(13) Ibid., p. 191.

12 The Unchained Lion

(1) Motely, *Rise of the Dutch republic*, vol. I, p. 67.

(2) Ibid., p. 68.

(3) Davis, *The voyages and works*, p. 128.

(4) Motely, *United Netherlands*, vol. III, p. 579.

(5) Ibid., vol. IV, p. 105.

(6) Ibid., p. 106.

(7) Ibid., p. 108.

(8) Ibid., pp. 132–34.

(9) Ibid.

(10) Schouten, *The relation of William Cornelison Schouten*, p. A.

(11) Ibid., p. 23.

(12) Ibid., p. 25.

(13) Motley, *United Netherlands*, vol. III, p. 579.

(14) Stavorinus, *Voyages to the East Indies*, vol. III, p. 396.

13 The Queen's Avenger

(1) Fletcher, p. 5.

(2) Ibid., p. 6.

(3) Ibid., p. 5.

(4) Ibid.

(5) Ibid., p. 7.

(6) Ibid., p. 28.

(7) Ibid., p. 30.

(8) Ibid., p. 34.

(9) Ibid., p. 8.

(10) Ibid., p. 39.

(11) Ibid., p. 62.

(12) Hakluyt, pp. 587–94.

(13) Fletcher, p. 11.

(14) Ibid., p. 84.

(15) Ibid., p. 89.

(16) Ibid.

(17) Hakluyt, pp. 208–12.

(18) Ibid., pp. 809–15.

14 John Company vs. Jan Compagnie

(1) Hakluyt, p. 252.

(2) Stavorinus, vol. I, p. 278.

(3) Roe, *Letters*, p. 662.

(4) Ibid., p. 664.

(5) Stavorinus, vol. II, pp. 409–10.

(6) Roe, *Letters*, p. 662.

(7) Ibid., p. 663.

(8) Ibid.

15 Factors—Theory and Practice

(1) Roe, *Letters*, p. 665.

(2) Stavorinus, vol. I, p. 312.

(3) Ibid., p. 313.

(4) Ibid., vol. III, p. 344.

(5) Banks, *The "Endeavour" journal*, vol. II, pp. 184, 232.

(6) Ibid.

(7) Stavorinus, vol. III, p. 396.

(8) Ibid., vol. II, p. 415.

(9) Morley, *Gladstone*, p. 256.

(10) Ibid.

(11) Stavorinus, vol. I, pp. 295–99.

16 Peter Pepper Has the Last Word

(1) Evelyn, *Diary*, vol. II, p. 75.

(2) Stavorinus, vol. II, pp. 130–31.

(3) Howe, p. 259.

(4) Stavorinus, vol. II, p. 331.

(5) Monardes, vol. I, p. 159.

Bibliography

Author's note: I attempt here to list all of the most significant works I have consulted and which a reader might find interesting. These include many works which have been translated from early accounts written in Dutch, Spanish, and Portuguese. Translator-editors of such books frequently include in their lengthy introductions other contemporary material of significance, e.g., included with Magellan's voyage are letters to the Portuguese king from his secret agent, Alvares, who was busily trying to have the voyage aborted.

Where books cited are collections of individual reports, e.g., *Tragic History of the Sea*, Hakluyt's *Principal Navigations*, I cite here both the collections and the individual reports. Where I cite a title in Spanish, any quotations I use have been my own translations. I do not include in my list encyclopedia articles, in various languages, or sketches in biographical dictionaries which I may have consulted in efforts to round out material consulted elsewhere or to seek out possible further

216 *Bibliography*

references to people whose works or adventures I attempt to follow.

Acosta, Padre Jose de. *Historia natural y moral de las Indias.* Mexico: Fondo de Cultura Economica, 1940.

Alboquerque, Afonso d'. *The commentaries of the great D'Alboquerque second viceroy of India.* London: Hakluyt Society, 1875.

Allan, J. T., Wolseley Haig, H. H. Dodwell, and R. R. Seth. *The Cambridge shorter history of India.* Delhi, India: S. Chand and Co., 1958.

Alvares, Francisco. *The Prester John of the Indies, a true relation of the lands of Prester John, being the narrative of the Portuguese embassy to Ethiopia in 1520, written by Father Alvares.* 2 volumes. Translated and edited by Lord Stanley of Alderley *1881), revised and edited by C. F. Beckingham and G. W. B. Huntingford. Cambridge: Cambridge University Press for the Hakluyt Society, 1961.

Amundsen, Roald. *The northwest passage: the "Gjoa" expedition, 1903–1907.* 2 vols. New York: E. P. Dutton Co., 1908.

Azurara, Gomes Eannes de. *Discovery and conquest of Guinea.* 2 volumes. Edited by C. R. Beasley and E. Prestage. Series I, Nos 95. and 100. Cambridge: Cambridge University Press, 1896, 1899.

Banks, Joseph. *The "Endeavour" journal of Joseph Banks, 1768–1771.* 2 vols. Edited by J. C. Beaglehole. Sydney: Public Library of New South Wales in association with Angua and Robertson, 1962.

Benavente, Fray Toribio de. *Historia de los Indios de la Nueva España.* Mexico: Salvador Chavez Hayhoe, 1941.

The book of a thousand nights and one night. 4 volumes. Translated by R. F. Burton and edited by L. C. Smithers. Volume II: *5th voyage of Sinbad the Seaman.* New York: privately printed, undated.

Boxer, C. R., ed. *The tragic history of the sea.* Cambridge:

Cambridge University Press for the Hakluyt Society, 1959.

Boxer, C. R., ed. *Further selections from the tragic history of the sea.* Cambridge: Cambridge University Press for the Hakluyt Society, 1968.

Boxer, C. R., ed. *South China in the sixteenth century being the narratives of Galeote Pereira, Fr. Gaspar da Cruz, O. P. & Fr. Martín de Rada (1550–1575).* London: Hakluyt Society, 1953.

Bradford, Ernle. *Southward the caravels: the story of Henry the Navigator.* London: Hutchinson, 1961.

Cabot, John. "Letters patent of King Henry the seventh unto John Cabot and his three sonnes, Lewis, Sebastian, and Sancius for the discoverie of new and unknowne lands, 1495." In *Principall navigations, voiages and discoveries of the English nation*, by Richard Hakluyt. Cambridge: Cambridge University Press for the Hakluyt Society, 1965.

Cabot, Sebastian. "A discourse of Sebastian Cabot touching his discoverie of the part of the West India out of England in the time of King Henry the Seventh." In *Principall navigations, voiages and discoveries of the English nation*, by Richard Hakluyt. Cambridge: Cambridge University Press for the Hakluyt Society, 1965.

Cameron, Ian. *Magellan and the first circumnavigation of the world.* New York: Saturday Review Press, 1973.

Chancellor, Richard. "The newe navigation and discoverie of the kingdom of Moscovia, by the northeast, in the yeere 1553, by Sir Hugh Willoughbie, knight, and performed by Richard Chancellor, Pilot maior of the voyage. Translated out of the latine into English." In *Principall navigations, voiages and discoveries of the English nation*, by Richard Hakluyt. Cambridge: Cambridge University Press for the Hakluyt Society, 1965.

Chapman, Laurence. "Letter from Laurence Chapman in Casbin, Persia, to worshipful merchant of the companie of Russia in London, Apr. 28, 1569." In *Principall navi-*

gations, voiages and discoveries of the English nation, by Richard Hakluyt. Cambridge: Cambridge University Press for the Hakluyt Society, 1965.

Chilton, John. "A notable discourse of Master John Chilton thouching . . . memorable things of the West Indies." In *Principall navigations, voiages and discoveries of the English nation,* by Richard Hakluyt, Cambridge: Cambridge University Press for the Hakluyt Society, 1965.

Columbus, Fernando. "The offer of the discoverie of the West Indies by Christopher Columbus to King Henrie the seventh in the yeare 1488." In *Principall navigations, voiages and discoveries of the English nation,* by Richard Hakluyt. Cambridge: Cambridge University Press for the Hakluyt Society, 1965.

Cook, James. *The voyage of the "Endeavour," 1768–1771.* Edited by J. C. Beaglehole. Cambridge University Press for the Hakluyt Society, 1955.

Colección de documentos inéditos relativos al descubrimiento, Conquista y organización de las antiguas posessiones espanoles de Ultramar. 1886.

Couto, Diogo de. "Narrative of the shipwreck of the great ship *São Thomas* in the land of the Fumos, in the year 1589." In *The tragic history of the sea,* edited by C. R. Boxer. Cambridge: Cambridge University Press for the Hakluyt Society, 1959.

Couto, Diogo de. "Narrative of the loss of the Aguia and Garca, 1559–1560." In *Further selections from the tragic history of the sea,* edited by C. R. Boxer. Cambridge: Cambridge University Press for the Hakluyt Society, 1968.

Dampier, William. *A new voyage round the world.* Edited by Percy G. Adams. New York: Dover, 1968.

Davis, John. *The voyages and works of John Davis, the navigator.* Edited by Albert H. Markham. London: Hakluyt Society, 1880.

Días del Castillo, Bernal. *La conquista de la Nueva España y Guatemala.* Volumes 9 and 10. Guatemala: Bibliotheca "Goathemala," 1933.

Dos Passos, John. *The Portugal story: three centuries of exploration and discovery.* Garden City: Doubleday & Co., 1969.

Edwards, Arthur. "Letters to the worshipfull companie trading with Russia, Persia . . . 1565–1567." In *Principall navigations, voiages and discoveries of the English nation,* by Richard Hakluyt. Cambridge: Cambridge University Press for the Hakluyt Society, 1965.

Evelyn, John. *The diary of John Evelyn.* 2 volumes. Edited by William Bray. London: M. Walter Dunne, 1901.

Fletcher, Francis. *The world encompassed by Sir Francis Drake.* Facsimile of 1628 edition with introduction by A. L. Rowse. Cleveland: Bibliotheca Americana, World Publishing Co., 1966.

Forrest, Thomas. *A voyage to New Guinea and the Moluccas from Balambangan.* London: G. Scott, 1779. Republished by Oxford, 1969.

Galvano, Antonio de. *The discoveries of the world from the first original unto the year of our Lord 1555 (1601) by Antonio Galvão, governor of Ternate.* English translation by R. Hakluyt. Series 1, No. 30. London: Hakluyt Society, 1862.

Gama, Vasco da. *The three voyages of Vasco da Gama and his viceroyalty.* Translated and edited by Henry E. J. Stanley. London: Hakluyt Society, 1898.

Gerard, John. *The herball or generall historie of plantes . . . very much enlarged and amended by Thomas Johnson, citizen and apothecarye of London.* London: Adam Islip, Joice Norton and Richard Whitakers, 1633. Republished, New York: Dover, 1975.

Gibbon, Edward. *Decline and fall of the Roman empire.* 3 volumes. New York: Heritage Press, 1946.

Griffiths, Percival. *The history of the Indian tea industry*. London: Weidenfeld and Hutchinson, 1967.

Guillemard, F. H. H. *The life of Ferdinand Magellan and the first circumnavigation of the globe*. London: 1890.

Hakluyt, Richard. *Principall navigations, voiages and discoveries of the English nation*. 2 volumes. Republished with introduction and index. Cambridge: Cambridge University Press for the Hakluyt Society, 1965.

Herodotus of Halicarnassus. Translated by George Rawlinson and edited by Manuel Komroff. New York: Tudor Publishing Co., 1934.

Hopkirk, Peter. *Foreign devils on the silk road. The search for the lost cities and treasures of Chinese Central Asia*. London: John Murray Ltd., 1980.

Howe, Sonia. *In quest of spices*. London: Herbert Jenkins Ltd., 1946.

Hudson, Henry. *Henry Hudson the navigator. Original documents in which his career is recorded*. Edited by C. M. Asher. London: Hakluyt Society, 1860.

Jayne, K. G. *Vasco da Gama and his successors, 1460–1580*. New York: Barnes & Noble, 1970.

Jenkinson, M. Anthonie. "A compedious and briefe declaration of the journey of M. Anthonie Jenkinson from the famous citie of London into the lands of Persia." In *Principall navigations, voiages and discoveries of the English nation*, by Richard Hakluyt. Cambridge: Cambridge University Press for the Hakluyt Society, 1965.

Jourdian, John. *The Journal of John Jourdain, 1608–1617, describing his experiences in Arabia, India, and the Malay archipelago*. Edited by William Foster. London: Hakluyt Society, 1905.

Keeling, William and Thomas Bonner. *The East India Company journals of William Keeling and Thomas Bonner*. Edited by Michael Strachan and Boies Penrose. Minneapolis: University of Minnesota Press, 1971.

Knaplund, Paul. *Gladstone's foreign policy.* New York: Harper Bros., 1935.

Komroff, Manuel, ed. *Contemporaries of Marco Polo consisting of the travel records to the eastern parts of the world of William of Rubruck (1253–1255); the journey of John Pian de Carpini (1245–1247); the journal of Friar Odoric (1318–1330) & the oriental travels of Rabbi Benjamin of Tudela (1160–1173).* London: Jonathan Cape, 1920.

Lamb, Harold. *The Crusades: the flame of Islam.* New York: Doubleday, Doran and Co., 1950.

Lancaster, James. *The voyages of James Lancaster to the East Indies.* Edited by Clements H. Markham. London: Hakluyt Society, 1877.

Las Casas, Bartolomé. *Historia de las Indias.* Edited by Augustin Millares Carlo y Lewis Hanke. Mexico: Fondo de Cultura Economico, 1965.

Lattimore, Owen. *Inner Asian frontiers of China.* New York: American Geographical Society, 1940.

Letts, Malcolm, ed. *Mandeville's travels, texts and translations.* 2 volumes. London: Hakluyt Society, 1953.

Linschoten, Jan Huyghen van. *The voyage of Jan Huyghen van Linschoten to the East Indies, from the old English translation of 1598.* Edited by A. C. Burnell. London: Hakluyt Society, 1885.

Ly-Tio-Fane, Madeleine. *The triumph of Jean Nicolas Céré and his Isle Bourdon collaborators (Mauritius and the spice trade).* Paris: Mouton & Cie., 1970.

Martins, J. P. Oliveira. *The golden age of Prince Henry the navigator.* English translation, 1914.

Merriman, Roger B. *The rise of the Spanish empire in the old world and in the new.* 4 volumes. New York: Macmillan Co.

Middleton, Henry. *The voyage of Sir Henry Middleton to Bantam and the Maluca Islands in 1606.* London: Hakluyt Society, 1856.

Mitchell, Mairin. *Friar Andres de Urdaneta O.S.A. (1508–1568), pioneer of Pacific navigation from west to east.* London: Macdonald & Evans Ltd., 1964.

Morga, Antonio de. *Sucesos de las Islas Filipinas.* Translated and edited by J. S. Cummins. London: Hakluyt Society, 1868.

Morison, Samuel Eliot. *Admiral of the ocean sea: a life of Christopher Columbus.* Boston: Little, Brown & Co., 1942.

Morison, Samuel Eliot, ed. *Journals and other documents on the life and voyages of Christopher Columbus.* New York: Heritage Press, 1971.

Morison, Samuel Eliot. *The European discovery of America: the northern voyages* A.D. *500–1600.* New York: Oxford University Press, 1971.

Morison, Samuel Eliot. *The European discovery of America: the southern voyages* A.D. *1492–1616.* New York: Oxford University Press, 1974.

Morley, John. *The Life of William Ewart Gladstone.* 3 volumes. London: Macmillan & Co., 1903.

Motley, John Lothrop. *Rise of the Dutch republic.* 2 volumes. A. L. Burt, undated.

Motley, John Lothrop. *History of the United Netherlands.* 4 volumes. New York: Harper Bros., 1868.

Newberie, John. "Letters by John Newberie sent from Aleppo, Babylon, Ormuz, Goa." In *Principall navigations, voiages and discoveries of the English nation,* by Richard Hakluyt. Cambridge: Cambridge University Press for the Hakluyt Society, 1965.

Nordenskiöld, A. E. *The voyage of the "Vega" round Asia and Europe with a historical review of previous journeys along the north coast of the old world.* 2 volumes. Translated by A. Leslie. London: Macmillan & Co., 1881.

"Notes concerning the trade in Alexandria (158?)." In *Principall navigations, voiages and discoveries of the English nation,* by Richard Hakluyt. Cambridge: Cambridge University Press for the Hakluyt Society, 1965.

Nowell, Charles E. *History of Portugal.* Englewood Cliffs, NJ: Prentice-Hall, 1953.

Nowell, Charles E. *Magellan's voyage around the world. Three contemporary accounts.* Evanston: Northwestern University Press, 1962.

Pearson, M. N. *Coastal western India. Studies from the Portuguese records.* New Delhi: Concept, 1981.

Pigafetta, Antonio Francesco. *The first voyage around the world.* Edited by Lord Stanley of Alderley. London: Hakluyt Society, 1874.

Pliney the Elder. *Natural History.* 10 volumes. Translated and edited by H. Rackham. Cambridge, MA: Wm. Heinemann Ltd., 1944–1953.

Polo, Marco. *Travels of Marco Polo, the Venetian.* Edited by T. Wright (1824) and published with an introduction by John Masefield. New York: E. P. Dutton, 1926.

Prescott, William H. *History of the conquest of Mexico.* 3 volumes. Edited by J. F. Kirk. Philadelphia: J. B. Lippincott Co., 1843.

Pyrard de Laval, Francois. *The voyage of Pyrard de Laval to the East Indies, the Maldives, the Moluccas and Brazil.* 2 volumes. Translated from the 3rd French edition of 1619 and edited by A. Gray and H. C. P. Bell. London: Hakluyt Society, 1887–1890.

Roe, Thomas. *The embassy of Sir Thomas Roe to the court of the Great Mogul, 1615–1619.* 2 volumes. Edited by William Foster. Oxford: Oxford University Press for the Hakluyt Society, 1926.

Roe, Thomas. *Journal and letters.* London: Lintot & Osborne, 1752.

Roncière, Charles de la and G. Clerc-Rampal. *Histoire de la Marine Francaise.* Paris: Librarie Larousse, 1934.

Schouten, William Cornelison. *The relation of William Corneli-son Schouten of Horne shewing how south from the Straights of Magelan, in Terra del-fuego, he found and discovered a newe passage through the great South Sea, and that way sayled around the world.* Facsimile of 1619 edition. Cleveland: World Publishing Co., 1966.

Schurz, William Lytle. *The Manila galleon.* New York: E. P. Dutton, 1959.

Skrine, Clarmont Festival. *Chinese central Asia.* London: Methuen & Co., 1926.

Stavorinus, Jan Splinter. *Voyages to the East Indies . . . 1768–1771.* 3 volumes. Translated and edited by Samuel Hull Wilcocke. London: Dawsons of Pall Mall, 1969.

Thorne, Robert. "Letter to Henry VIII." In *Principall navigations, voiages and discoveries of the English nation,* by Richard Hakluyt. Cambridge: Cambridge University Press for the Hakluyt Society, 1965.

Ukers, William H. *All about tea.* 2 volumes. New York: Tea & Coffee Trade Journal Co., 1935.

Veer, Gerrit de. *The three voyages of William Barents to the Arctic regions (1594, 1595, 1596).* Edited by Koolemans Beynen. London: Hakluyt Society, 1876.

Villiers, A. J. de, ed. *The East and West Indian mirror, being an account of Joris van Spielbergen's voyage around the world, 1614–1617 and the Australian navigations of Jacob le Maire.* London: Hakluyt Society, 1906.

Walter, Richard. *A voyage round the world in the years 1740–1744 by George Anson, Commander in Chief of a squadron of His Majesty's ships, sent upon an expedition to the South Seas.* Everyman's Library, 1911.

Williamson, J. A., ed. *The Cabot voyages and Bristol discovery under Henry VII.* Cambridge: Cambridge University Press for the Hakluyt Society, 1961.

Willoughby, Westel W. *Opium as an international problem: the*

Geneva conferences. Baltimore: The Johns Hopkins Press, 1925.

Wright, Ione S. *Voyages of Saavedra Ceron.* Miami: University of Miami Hispanic Studies, 1951.

Wroth, Lawrence C. *The voyages of Giovanni Verrazzano, 1524–1528.* New Haven: Yale University Press, 1970.

Index

236   *Index*